The Proverb Effect

The Proverb Effect

*Secrets to creating tiny phrases
that change the world*

RON PLOOF

For Dad. I miss you every day.

Table of Contents

Introduction

Let's try an experiment. Finish the following phrase:

If at first you don't succeed...

How'd you do? Did you say...*try, try again?*

I've performed this experiment hundreds of times and the results defy conventional wisdom. While professional communicators toil relentlessly to craft messages for recall hours, days, or even months later, this eighteenth-century phrase has occupied our collective memories for more than ten generations.

But, how did it happen? How is it possible for some messages to survive decades, centuries, or in rare instances, millennia? For example:

If the gloves don't fit, you must acquit (Cochran, 1995)
Actions speak louder than words (Lincoln, 1856)
Slow and steady wins the race (Aesop, ~550 BC)

The answer is found in proverbs, perfectly crafted phrases that have successfully passed wisdom from generation to generation, independent of time, culture, or creed. Proverbs are the ultimate long-stories short, and while it's easy to dismiss them as droll or trite, doing so just underestimates the complexity by which they facilitate both human understanding and communications. Proverbs draw their power from the simplicity of their presentation.

I wrote this book to help you use the power of proverbs to become a better communicator. Read it to learn:

- Why proverbs reign supreme over other message types
- What makes proverbs the triple-threat of communications: memorable, repeatable and most importantly, persuasive
- A step-by-step methodology to apply the most powerful communications device in human history

Want to learn how to harness the timeless and universal power of proverbs? Then I've got a story for you.

Ron Ploof
November 5, 2018

The Proverb

A spark can start a great fire

It had been three years since the sound of applause emanated from Atamaq's quarterly All-hands meeting. Weary employees, beaten down by twelve consecutive quarters of cost-cutting justifications finally saw the chart that they'd all been waiting for—one with more black than red and a steep revenue forecast that stretched up-and-to-the-right.

"It's a classic feast or famine situation," Atamaq's CEO, Craig said. "Six months ago, we struggled to keep the lights on and today we find ourselves understaffed. As a result, I'm here to make three announcements. First, I'm lifting the hiring moratorium."

The audience applauded.

"Second, we need to accelerate our hiring process.

So, I've just reauthorized the company's employee referral bonus program."

The audience applauded a little more enthusiastically.

"And before I make my last announcement, I want to thank each of you for hanging with us through these difficult times. Not only have we lost friends and colleagues due to layoffs, but we've also lost some of our traditions. Three years ago, we mothballed our Diamonds in Seven showcase," he said, referring to the company's tradition of encouraging Atamaq's up-and-comers to present their work in seven minutes or less. "But I'm pleased to announce that the Di7 tradition returns today. So, without further ado, let me introduce the first of our two presenters. The floor is yours, Justin."

Justin had waited a long time for this moment. Had Atamaq's financial situation been healthier, it would have happened two years ago. But here he was, demonstrating his ability to make any subject entertaining through his offbeat sense of humor. The audience hung on his every word as he presented what should have been a mind-numbing analysis of daily-rates vs. customer-satisfaction scores. He finished his seven-minute presentation on the dot with, "Just remember, if you wanna pay peanuts, hire a monkey."

The audience bellowed.

"Any questions?" he asked.

Samantha Kim couldn't hear Justin's Q&A over the din of her beating heart. Atamaq's youngest project manager hated following Justin. He was everything that she wasn't: dynamic, informative, and fun.

"Anything else?" Justin asked after the last question. "Great, then I'll hand the mic over to Sam, who'll guide us through the riveting topic of schedule analysis." The audience howled as Justin feigned falling asleep.

"Thank you, Justin," Sam lied. "Today I'm presenting my regression analysis on enterprise-wide schedule-slipping." She peppered the crowd with charts, graphs, and tables. She discussed correlations, predictions, and covariance equations. Heads bobbed throughout the room as audience members struggled to stay awake. Just as she was about to conclude, a loud pop interrupted her soliloquy.

"Saved by the bell," Justin commented on the exploding projector bulb. The audience appreciated the much-needed moment of levity.

Sam's boss, Ryan, quelled the audience. "Okay. Quiet down. Sam, do you need us to get a new projector?"

While she appreciated her boss's rescue attempt, Sam decided to let her audience off the hook. "No, I was almost done anyway. Are there any questions?"

Crickets. *Of course*, Sam thought. *Who'd want to ask the nerd girl about her analysis?*

Justin broke the awkward silence. "Thanks, Sam," he said, midstride toward the door. The rest of the audience followed him.

"Well, that was unfortunate," Ryan said.

"The presentation or the bulb explosion?"

"The bulb. C'mon, Sam. So, your presentation was a little rocky. That's to be expected. You've been at this for what, a few months?"

"I knew all of the information," she protested. "Cold."

"That's the easy part. Now you need to find better ways of connecting with your audience. Think back to the part where Justin presented..."

"Do I have to?" she interrupted.

"I know that Justin's a little smug, but..."

"...a little?"

"...and he has an ego..."

"…the size of a house…"

"…but people want to hear what he's saying, Sam. He's entertaining."

"Is that it?" she asked incredulously. "All I need to do is learn how to be funny?"

"That's not what I'm saying. Funny is his thing. You've got to find yours."

Ryan was right. Sam understood the business, the people, and how to translate that understanding into computer models. But she hadn't yet figured out how to convey what she knew. She truly needed to find her thing.

"You'll figure it out," Ryan said. "Just give it some time."

"How much?" Sam asked. "At this rate, I'll have it all worked out by my retirement party."

CADE LOOKED AROUND the coffee shop while waiting for Sam. The Ph.D. candidate in philosophy saw a teenage couple paying more attention to their cell phones than to one another. He studied his subjects with fascination. They represented a new generation that seemed more interested in interacting with their personal media devices than with the living beings sitting across from them. He was so caught up in his thoughts that he didn't hear Sam arrive.

"Hello? Earth to Cade," she said. She'd seen this Cade before—the one who was so fixated on something that if she wasn't careful, she'd be sucked unwillingly into a deep discussion about whatever was rattling around in his overly-dramatic noggin. Her only chance at having a normal conversation this morning hinged on her ability to disrupt his present fixation. She had an idea—a somewhat drastic one, she thought—but desperate times justified desperate measures.

Sam reached over and ever-so-lightly touched the hair behind his ear. Cade's response was instantaneous and explosive as he jumped out of his seat, yelped an expletive, and proceeded to perform a spastic shimmy-dance. All eyes in the café turned toward him, including those of the pretty barista behind the counter.

"What the hell did you do that for, Sam? You know how much I hate spiders!"

"Sorry. I tried saying hello, but you didn't hear me."

"Couldn't you find a nicer way of getting my attention—like hitting me over the head with a baseball bat?"

Sam comforted him with a friendly hug. "How are you?" she asked.

"I was fine until you sent my blood pressure through the roof." He pointed across the room. "I was just watching those two over there."

Sam tried not to look. Although her fake spider trick had failed, she wasn't giving up. She needed to remain disengaged at this pivotal moment. If she took the bait, she'd be sucked into *the conversation* about Cade's pet peeve—people engrossed in their screens while ignoring life. "So, how are your folks doing?" she asked in a valiant attempt to change the subject.

Cade continued to stare. "What do you think they're searching for?" he asked.

Sam remained steadfast in her avoidance. "Your folks?"

"My folks? What? No. Sam, I'm talking about those kids over there with their noses buried in their devices. What do you think they're searching for?"

"Perhaps they're trying to find a movie?" Sam deadpanned.

"A movie? Are you kidding me? That would require some form of interaction. They're totally absorbed in their own virtual worlds, swallowed up into the digital realm of endless stimulation!"

The pretty barista looked up, smiled, and went back to work on a mocha cappuccino.

Sam tried one last time to change the subject. "I take it the dissertation isn't going well?"

"My advisor doesn't like my topics. She wants me to be more specific!"

"Okay," Sam said softly. "Time to use your inside voice."

Cade slumped in his chair. He knew that his theories flirted with fanaticism and Sam was one of the only people who'd call him on it. "I'm sorry. I'm just under a lot of pressure. My advisor keeps stomping on my proposals and I'm running out of time."

Sam pointed to the young couple. "How much more specific can you get than that? You just went on a tirade about how our communications devices keep us from communicating. Maybe you should try something like…"

"Not specific enough," he snipped.

"Then, let's narrow it down. If these new technologies have inhibited our ability to communicate, doesn't that mean that we used to be better communicators?"

"Maybe."

"So, humor me. If we've lost this ability, how do we get it back?"

Cade appreciated how Sam could always keep him grounded. "Thanks, Sam. I needed that."

"That's my job," she said.

"Lemme think about your questions, but first, I need to take care of something." Cade stood and started walking toward the teenagers.

"Where are you going?" Sam asked rhetorically, knowing exactly what he was up to.

"Hi," Cade said to the boy.

The boy looked up, dumbfounded.

"You see her?" Cade said, pointing to the kid's table mate.

"Yeah?" the boy responded.

"Just talk to her."

Sam tugged at Cade's arm. "C'mon, Cupid. It's time to leave."

"Try putting down the screen. Ask about her day. Tell her about yours."

The girl looked up from her own phone to find herself as the center of attention. Her gaze ping-ponged between spastic-dance guy and her confused-looking friend.

Sam tugged harder. "Cade. You're starting to sound like a crazy person." She used the awkward moment of silence as an opportunity to wheel Cade toward the front door. "Feel better?" she asked as they exited the café.

"Much," he said.

SAM AWOKE TO the most annoying wake-up song that she could find on her cell phone app. She swatted clumsily toward the noise to make it stop then surveyed the room for any clue as to where she was. Then she remembered—San Francisco—and her flight home was scheduled to leave in three hours.

It had been a month since the exploding projector bulb incident. Ryan sent her to the conference to pick up some communications skills. Although she hadn't yet found her thing, she did find herself reviewing some new techniques while riding the elevator down to the hotel's lobby.

The elevator's descent slowed to stop at another floor. "Good morning," a woman said as she pulled her roller-suitcase over the elevator's threshold.

Sam's heart raced as she recognized Tina Hailey-Jowett, yesterday's keynote speaker. "G...Good morning," Sam said, stumbling over her words. She tried to meet Tina after her talk, but one of the conference's handlers had rescued her from an ever-growing line of well-wishers. But now, alone with Tina in the elevator, Sam couldn't muster the nerve to approach her.

Tina leaned against the wall and waited for the elevator to continue its downward trek. Another suitcase-toting traveler recognized her immediately. "Good morning, Ms. Jowett. I really enjoyed your talk yesterday," he said.

Dammit, Sam thought. *Why couldn't I have done that?*

"Thank you," Tina said before testing his sincerity. "What was your favorite part?"

"I really liked when you said, *at a round table there's no dispute about the place.* It reminded me of a problem that we're having at work. We had a reorg. Instead of listening to one another, everyone's jockeying for their next position. That statement got me thinking about ways to help my team feel less threatened."

Tina appreciated his situation. "Workplace politics are tough," Tina said. "Good luck."

The elevator doors opened on the ground floor. The man headed for the front desk while Tina and

11

Sam proceeded toward the hotel exit. Just as Tina was about to walk through the revolving door, Sam screwed up her courage and touched Tina's arm.

"Ms. Jowett!" Sam said a bit too loudly.

Tina recoiled. "Yes?"

"I'm so sorry, but I too wanted to say how much I enjoyed your presentation."

Tina recognized Sam as the shy girl from the elevator. "Thank you. What's your name?"

"Sam," she said.

"Nice to meet you, Sam. Please call me Tina."

Sam stared at her awkwardly, not knowing what to say next. Tina broke the silence. "What can I do for you, Sam?"

"You're such a good presenter. I hope to be that good someday."

Tina smiled. "It just takes practice. All you need to do is…" The buzz of Tina's cell phone interrupted her sentence. "I'm sorry, Sam. But my limo's right over there."

Sam had come too far to end the conversation. "What were you about to say? Something about all I need to do is…"

"…learn the secrets of proverbs," Tina said as

she handed her suitcase to the limo driver.

"Secrets?" Sam asked, locking eyes with Tina in a feeble attempt to freeze this pivotal moment for as long as she could.

Tina had seen this same expression twenty years ago while looking into a mirror. She wondered if it was the one that convinced Mr. Kemper to take her under his wing. "Where are you off too?" Tina asked.

"SFO."

Tina wondered. Perhaps it was time to start sharing Mr. Kemper's wisdom with the next generation. "Me too," she said. "Want a lift?"

Sam hesitated, trying to wrap her head around this unexpected twist.

Tina pointed to the open limo door. "Fortune favors the bold, Sam."

And with that, Sam slid in. The two women sat in silence as the limo inched its way through heavy San Francisco traffic before Sam turned and asked, "Proverbs?"

"Proverbs are little nuggets of wisdom. They're special because they convey deep meaning, spread easily, and are repeatable."

"Like?"

"Finish the following sentence for me: Don't put off for tomorrow what you…"

"…can do today?" Sam answered.

"That's a proverb. Its roots go back to Chaucer in the late 1300s[1]."

"The late 1300s?" Sam said. "I can't get people to remember what I said yesterday."

Tina laughed. "That's why you should learn how proverbs work, when to use them, and ultimately how to create your own."

"I came to this conference to develop my presentation skills. Will proverbs help me do that?"

"Not only will they make you a better presenter, Sam, but they'll make you a better communicator. You'll speak more clearly and with a purpose."

That's all Sam ever wanted. She had big ideas and wanted to share them in the most effective way. "Hey! You used a proverb to get me into the limo."

"*Fortune favors the bold.* See how effective proverbs are? They simultaneously convey meaning and create

---

[1] Gregory Titelman, America's Popular Proverbs and Sayings (New York: Random House, 2000), 241.

calls-to-action."

"I'd never heard that saying before, but somehow understood exactly what it meant."

"That's how proverbs work. They contain the DNA of wisdom. There's something about the way they're built that entices the listener's brain to extract more meaning than the actual words used to construct them."

"Sounds complicated."

"It's simpler than you might think after you understand the basics." Tina's cell phone buzzed once again. She looked at its screen and frowned.

"Problem?" Sam asked.

"Flight's delayed. Looks I'm stuck here a little longer."

Sam's phone buzzed. "Hmm. What flight are you on?"

"The 9:25 to Chicago."

Sam held up her phone to show its screen. "Ditto."

The Benefit Rule

It is better to give than receive

The more Cade listened to the Advisor the more frustrated he felt. "But, it's about communication," he protested.

"You keep saying that, Cade, but whenever I ask for specifics, you spin off in different directions. First, it was societal evolution, then it was early education, and today it's technology. Don't get me wrong, all are great topics for your dissertation, but you must settle on one."

Although he didn't want to admit it, he knew she was right. He always had too many ideas and could never choose between them. Sam called it the tyranny of choice because selecting one meant eliminating another. But the Advisor didn't see it that way. Most of Cade's topics shared a common thread: how humans passed knowledge from one generation to another. He just needed a nudge.

"Let's try this another way. How do humans pass knowledge between each other?"

"Through language and actions," Cade said.

"At the high level, sure. But what about the process?"

"Technology has changed the process."

The Advisor shook her head. "We've been down this road before, Cade."

Cade took a deep breath. He needed to stop feeling defensive and let the Advisor help him. "Okay. When humans developed the ability to communicate verbally, I'm wondering if we stumbled upon specific words that resonated with our natural cognitive abilities."

The Advisor appreciated Cade's lack of defensiveness. "What kind of words?"

"To be honest, I don't know."

"I don't believe that. What's your gut telling you?"

Cade drummed his fingers on his notebook. "I think it might have something to do with now. The present. People are much more accepting when new information helps solve an immediate problem."

"So, it sounds like you're looking for a connection between linguistics, time, and the transfer of wisdom?"

Wisdom, Cade thought. Up until this point, he'd been describing his problem in terms of knowledge-transfer, but the Advisor's use of the word *wisdom* changed everything. "I like that," he said. "What if I work on wisdom-transfer this week?"

"And when you say work on wisdom," the Advisor cajoled, "do you mean, returning with deeper insight, or just bringing me yet another topic?"

Cade raised his hand playfully. "I promise to stay on topic, the whole topic and nothing but the topic, so help me God."

"Okay, then," the Advisor laughed. "Let me know if you need any more help."

SAM'S BOSS, RYAN, listened to his voicemail.

"Hi Ryan, this is Amy over at Pentameter. We need to speak. Can you give me a call on my cell? It's important."

Ryan stared at his phone and wondered what could be so important. Not only was Pentameter Atamaq's oldest client, but the two companies were about to ink their largest deal, a multi-million-dollar contract to develop Pentameter's next product line.

Atamaq had just hired an entire team in anticipation for starting project Santiago as early as next week. Ryan tapped Amy's number into his desk phone. She answered in two rings.

"Good morning, Ryan," Amy answered. "Thanks for returning my call."

"Anytime. What's up?"

"Actually, this is a courtesy call. We've worked with each other for a long time and I thought that we should speak in person." Amy paused to get the words right. "There's no easy way to say this, Ryan, so I'm just gonna blurt it out. I've decided to give our business to Zenekas."

Ryan felt a knot form in his stomach. "Umm…" was the best response he could muster.

"This can't be a surprise, Ryan. We've been expressing our dissatisfaction for months. Our customers are demanding tighter schedules and we've been asking you for ways to meet their needs. Every time we ask for new ideas, your project managers lecture us on why it's impossible. You need to know that while they were lecturing, Zenekas was presenting us with some radical new ideas."

"But, Amy. They'll say anything to…"

"...which is why I asked them to put their money where their mouth is," she finished his sentence. "You know project Shawsheen—the one that your company claimed couldn't be completed in under a year? Zenekas just delivered it in six months."

"But..."

"Ryan, we've enjoyed a great relationship. Our company wouldn't be where it is today without Atamaq's help. But, we need the latest tools and the latest processes. Atamaq doesn't have what we need and Zenekas does."

"And Santiago?"

"I'm sorry, Ryan."

Ryan's mind raced. Atamaq had taken a big risk hiring in advance of this contract. He had to try one more time. "Is there anything I can do to change your mind?"

"I'm sorry. It's done, Ryan."

And with that, Ryan stared at the phone and wondered how he'd break the news to his volatile CEO.

THE WAITING AREA outside of Gate 57 bustled with activity. Business people talked on their phones, teenagers hoarded the power outlets, and gate agents helped customers with their various issues. Sam looked through the window to see air where an airplane ought to be. The monitor behind the counter informed those waiting that the flight to Chicago was delayed for an hour.

"How did you get into proverbs?" Sam asked before taking a sip of her French Roast.

"An old friend introduced them to me," Tina said. "I had a paper route as a teenager and loved spending time with one of my customers. Mr. Kemper was a retired engineer and he always had a unique perspective on things."

"Like?"

"Like, when my father lost his job due to technology, Mr. Kemper's advice got him back into the job market. Or, when I fretted over what classes to take in college, his wisdom guided me through the myriad of choices." Tina embraced warm memories of drinking tea at Mr. Kemper's kitchen table while listening to hundreds of his stories. He played a big role in her life.

"I've always wanted a mentor," Sam said. "Mr. Kemper sounds like a great guy."

"He taught me lots about life—most of it through proverbs. He got pretty sick at the end, but rather than lamenting, he told me, *Don't knock on death's door. Ring the doorbell and run.*"

Sam laughed. "He was funny!"

"You have no idea."

"And his connection to proverbs?"

"He collected them. He left me a notebook containing almost fifteen-hundred of them."

Sam's eyes widened. "Fifteen-hundred? So, I'm guessing that Mr. Kemper uncovered some secrets to proverbs?"

"Lots. Much of his work centered on why proverbs propagate so freely from person-to-person and generation-to-generation."

"And?"

"He believed that the driving force behind a proverb's proliferation was the motivation of the speaker. He called it The Benefit Rule because only the listener benefitted from the wisdom."

Sam didn't understand.

"First, let's look at some proverbs like *One man's trash is another man's treasure; Talking comes by nature, silence by wisdom; Hope for the best, plan for the worst.* It's obvious that each one means something to the listener, but what does the speaker get by sharing any of them?"

Sam stared back blankly.

Tina clarified. "In business, we create messages that serve an agenda—to persuade people to do something, such as buy a product, adopt an idea, or change a perspective. Therefore, most business messages are crafted to benefit the speaker."

"So, proverbs don't benefit speakers?"

"Mr. Kemper didn't think so. He believed that proverbs work their magic because the speaker expects nothing in return for sharing the wisdom."

"Nothing?"

"Think about it. What does a speaker gain from saying, *talking comes by nature, silence by wisdom?*"

Sam struggled with her answer. "Umm...nothing?" She started to see a connection. "So, proverbs are altruistic in nature?"

"Directly, yes, but there might be an indirect societal benefit. Proverb speakers may be motivated by the instinct to proliferate the species. By sharing wisdom, proverb speakers may be unconsciously ensuring that future generations receive vital advice."

Sam wondered about her own presentations. When she prepared, which did she emphasize? Did she put more emphasis on what she wanted to say or what her audience needed to hear?

A large shadow suddenly eclipsed the sunlight as a Boeing 737 crept toward Gate 57. "Looks like our ride has arrived," Sam said.

RYAN APPROACHED CEO CRAIG'S OFFICE with trepidation. Atamaq's top dog had neither the patience nor ability to react well to bad news.

"Enter!" Craig commanded in response to the knock on his door.

"Craig, I just got off the phone with Amy over at Pentameter."

Craig looked over the top of his reading glasses and smiled. "And how is our old friend doing?"

Ryan pulled the bandage off quickly. "She fired us."

Craig's face flushed red. "What the hell do you mean she fired us?" he screamed, the sound of his voice reverberating throughout the hallways. As she'd done many times before, Craig's admin closed his office door gingerly to muffle future and inevitable outbursts. "Who did we lose to?"

Telling Craig that they'd lost the account was the easy part. Telling him that they lost to their archrival would be the painful part. "Zenekas."

The vein running down the center of Craig's forehead pulsed with rage. "Zenekas? Zenekas couldn't find its way out of the city with a map! Is it recoverable?" he asked.

"It's not looking good," Ryan said

CEO Craig stood to use his six-foot-four-inch, two-hundred sixty-five-pound frame and Ryan's last name to punctuate his statement. "Fix it, Mr. Jones. Just fix it."

"My team's pulling together Pentameter's most recent CPs. Hopefully, we'll find something."

"Make it fast. I don't need to remind you of what this means to the company. This isn't just your job on the line, Mr. Jones. It's all of ours."

"Yes, sir. I'll get to the bottom of it."

"Damned straight you will," Craig said while reaching for his cell phone. "And so will I."

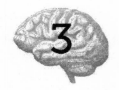

The Greeks

Learn from new books and old teachers

Cade liked how the Advisor replaced the word *knowledge* with *wisdom* because it helped him focus on the recipient's needs instead of the speaker's. Transferring knowledge required only facts, but transferring wisdom required something much deeper—the speaker must care about the listener. If wisdom came from experience and great wisdom came at the cost of pain, the motivation for sharing it required an empathy to spare others from experiencing the same misfortunes.

He scribbled questions into his notebook. Where did wisdom come from? Where was it kept? What's in it for us? The more he wrote, the more he realized that wisdom-transfer through language is what separated us from the beasts.

But how? What were the mechanics? How did the wisdom of a teacher nestle itself into the memories of a student? Why do we accept some advice and reject others? We're inundated with countless pieces of advice every day yet ignore most of it, so what makes one person's wisdom more appealing than another's? Finally, what persuades a recipient to not only accept the advice but to then execute it?

Cade wasn't the first person to wrestle with this problem. The Greeks had much to say about wisdom-transfer. He reached for his copy of Aristotle's *Rhetoric*, the twenty-three-hundred-year-old treatise that listed the three ingredients of persuasion: *logos*, *pathos*, and *ethos*. Perhaps it held a clue for him to follow?

Aristotle postulated that persuasion, the ability to turn someone's opinion, required no less than three components. *Ethos* referred to the character of the speaker and included things like trustworthiness, credibility, and respect. *Logos* referred to the data and logic behind the message. Finally, *pathos* referred to the emotional content of the message. Aristotle claimed that persuasion was an all-or-nothing proposition, thus it could only occur when a credible source delivered hard facts with human emotion. Without all three components, persuasion attempts will fail.

Cade saw evidence of this in academia. Most of his left-brained colleagues worshipped facts and dismissed emotion which obscured their ability to see the entire picture. And yet, the opposite was also true. Putting more stock into emotion over logic led to similar downfalls. Mathematician John Allen Paulos demonstrated how *innumerates*, a term he used to describe people with a limited understanding of numbers, rely too heavily on their emotions to make decisions.

He described the case of innumerates rationalizing the infinitesimally small odds of dying in a plane crash. They ...*inevitably respond with the non-sequitur, 'Yes, but what if you're that one,' and then nod knowingly, as if they've demolished your argument with their penetrating insight. This tendency to personalize is...a characteristic of many people who suffer from innumeracy.*[2]

Cade had a lot to think about. Too much faith in pure logic or pure emotion clouded our perceptions of reality. To persuade, speakers needed to choose words that resonated with both hemispheres of the listener's brain: the logical left and the emotional right. Could this be where he should narrow his focus?

He opened his notebook to a clean page and

---

[2] John Allen Paulos, Innumeracy: Mathematical Illiteracy and Its Consequences (New York: Vintage Books, 1988), 9-10.

started writing.

THE FLIGHT FROM San Francisco to Chicago had reached its cruising altitude, thus signaling the pilot's obligatory remarks. "Good morning ladies and gentlemen," a midwestern accent said from the cockpit. The voice apologized for the ground delay, promised to use a tailwind to make up some of the time, and then instructed passengers to sit back and enjoy the rest of their flight to the Windy City.

Somehow Tina had convinced the man in 12B to trade seats with Sam. Although she couldn't prove it, Sam surmised that it probably involved a proverb. "I'm really impressed with Mr. Kemper," Sam said, as she settled in. "He cared so much about his work."

"Mr. Kemper loved the pursuit of knowledge and had an insatiable need to understand how things worked. He once told me that he spent his entire career expressing the laws of nature through mathematical equations. In retirement, he hoped to understand the laws of human nature." Tina reached into her bag and pulled out a weathered, leather-bound notebook. "I think he got off to a great start with this."

Sam's eyes widened. "Is that what I think it is?"

she asked excitedly.

"The one and only," Tina confirmed as she handed it to Sam, "Mr. Kemper's notebook."

Sam held the leather-bound proverb collection as if she were holding the Book of Kells. She ran her palm across the soft leather cover before flipping through its yellowed pages. "There's a lot of work in here," she said.

"There is. And it's even more impressive considering that Mr. Kemper completed his analysis by hand. He didn't have access to the computational power that we have today. Unfortunately, this limitation kept him from his ultimate goal of creating a predictable way to construct proverbs."

A panicked expression appeared on Sam's face. Her career relied on becoming a better communicator and Tina had convinced her that the secret resided within these pithy statements. "He didn't?"

"No. He had lots of theories, but without computers, his focus was limited to a high level of abstraction. Luckily, I had no such limitations."

"So, you continued his work?"

"It was the least I could do. I've made it my life's mission to prove his theories."

"Like?"

"Mr. Kemper believed that proverbs rely on specific words to carry their wisdom—building blocks if you will. He believed that somehow these building blocks resonated with people, thus making proverbs easy to remember and proliferate. Have you ever heard of the Gunning FOG index?"

"Vaguely. I'm having uncomfortable flashbacks to my college freshman English class. Does it have something to do with the education level required to read a given text?"

"It does. I ran Mr. Kemper's proverb collection through a Gunning FOG analysis to learn that collectively, proverbs require a 4.76-grade level education to read." Tina then winked. "In other words, you don't need to be smarter than a fifth-grader to read proverbs."

"That's amazing!"

"It's even more amazing when comparing proverbs with other literary works such as *The Declaration of Independence*, *Pride & Prejudice*, or *The Red Badge of Courage*. When ranked next to forty-four of these other works, proverbs came in as the second-easiest to read."

"What came in first?" Sam asked.

"*The Cat in the Hat*, by Dr. Seuss, with a 2.95-grade reading level."

Sam laughed. "Of course."

"Wanna know what came in third at 5.95? *If you Give a Moose a Cookie* by Laura Joffe Numeroff."

"I love that book," Sam said. "I just read it to my nephew last week."

"For some reason, proverbs are easier to read than other works. Consider that you only need a 4.76-grade education to read a proverb, yet a post-graduate education to read *The US Declaration of Independence* at 20.48. Proverbs are easier to read than *The Adventures of Tom Sawyer* (7.87), *Treasure Island* (8.73,) and the *New York Times* (11.5)[3]. And if you want to know why teenagers are more interested in sex than civics, one needs a Ph.D. to read the *US Constitution* (17.22) while only an eleventh-grade education to read the *Kama Sutra*."

Sam laughed again. "That explains a lot."

"So, although Mr. Kemper never had a chance to prove it, his instincts were spot-on. The compact nature of proverbs speaks to the widest possible audience. Consider that the smallest proverb uses

---

[3] Data from pre-calculated LIWC values

two words; the largest uses twenty-three; and the median number of words used in Mr. Kemper's proverbs is seven."

"Wait," Sam said. "There's a two-word proverb?"

"Mr. Kemper collected eight of them, like *Accidents happen*; *Buyer beware*, and *Safety first*. And while we're on the subject of length, the largest proverb in Mr. Kemper's collection uses only one hundred twenty-nine characters—which means..." Tina paused to give time for Sam to answer.

Sam's eyes lit up. "...they're all tweetable!"

"Proverbs are short, sweet, and to the point. Mr. Kemper liked to call them the ultimate long-story-short."

"*Brevity is the soul of wit?*" Sam chided.

"Touché," the teacher said to her pupil.

Sam liked what Tina was telling her but felt something was missing. There had to be more to proverbs than just their readability and small size. "Tina? Is there something special about the way proverbs use these simple words?"

Tina pushed her seat back. "Absolutely. So far, we've looked at proverbs from a macro-view. It's now time to take a closer look at the actual words used to construct them."

FIVE HASTILY ASSEMBLED Atamaq managers gathered around the executive conference table. None knew why they were called to this emergency meeting, but all noticed that each attendee had one thing in common. All had worked on at least one Pentameter project. Speculative conversations echoed throughout the room on topics ranging from a corporate takeover to layoffs.

Ryan's entrance quelled the din. "This is a pen-down meeting," he said before hitting them with the news. "Pentameter fired us today."

The room filled with the sounds of gasps and sighs. It didn't take long for the dissonant cacophony to coalesce into a single question.

"So, is this a mass firing?" someone asked.

"No," Ryan said. "We're here to find out what went wrong and how to win them back."

"And if that doesn't work?" another manager asked.

"Let's napalm that bridge when we come to it," Ryan said. "I'd like to review Pentameter's most recent CPs."

A CP was Atamaq's internal name for a project review. Colloquially called postmortems, CEO Craig preferred the term Cow Pie, a reference to messy mistakes that project teams stepped into during an engagement. The goal was to learn from those mistakes and reduce the possibility of repeating them.

"I didn't have any Cow Pies on my last two projects," Justin said proudly.

"Me either," another seconded his motion.

That didn't sound right to Ryan. "Nobody had any CPs?"

"Normal project bumps and bruises," Justin said. "But nothing major."

"Then we've found our problem," Ryan said. "This is consistent with Amy's feedback. She said that we spent more time pushing schedules back than pushing them forward. If we weren't making mistakes, we probably weren't taking enough risks."

"We were trying to make the schedules predictable," Justin protested.

"And in doing so, we likely eliminated all risk," Ryan replied.

"And that's a bad thing?"

Ryan spread some papers across the conference table. "Longer schedules are easier schedules. Let me ask the question another way. How many schedules did we hit, come in under, and come in over?"

"They all hit," seemed to be the consensus.

"Then, I rest my case," Ryan said.

"They're firing us for hitting all of our schedules?" Justin asked.

"I would've," Ryan said. "One last thing. Can someone call up Pentameter's customer satisfaction reports for the past year?"

Justin projected his tablet onto the conference room's screen. Ryan saw that the problem was hidden in clear sight. Although Pentameter had rated all Atamaq's work as "Satisfied," the free-form answers foreshadowed their present situation. All referenced a desire to shorten schedules.

"The clues were there all along," Ryan said, "and we ignored them. I ignored them! We were so proud of the flawless success rate that we ignored our client's requests. That's why Pentameter fired us."

The room fell silent.

"Okay," Ryan said. "I know that this is a big shock and you probably need time to process this information, but I want you to review your old projects for ways that we could have shortened schedules." Blank stares indicated that they still didn't understand. "I'm only looking for your most creative ideas. Don't bring me anything that doesn't have the potential to cut a project schedule in half."

"Half?" Justin said. "That's impossible, Ryan."

"Not for Zenekas. They did so on Shawsheen and are now applying those same techniques to Santiago."

"I didn't think that Santiago had started yet," Justin said.

"It did," Ryan said. "Just not with us."

CADE KNEW THAT the missing piece had something to do with language. At some time in ancient history, humans developed the ability to share ideas verbally. But how? While Aristotle described the process of persuasion, the famous philosopher fell short of assembling a precise method for presenting ethos, logos, and pathos. But Aristotle's teacher, Plato, did.

Plato had developed a way to share complicated ideas through a story-form called *allegory*. Allegories taught lessons through contrived situations yet were familiar enough for listeners to relate. He used his most recognized work, *The Allegory of the Cave*[4] to

---

[4] https://www.youtube.com/watch?v=1RWOpQXTltA

demonstrate what it felt like to be a philosopher among non-philosophers.

Cade felt a kinship with Plato. By choosing a career in philosophy, he instantly became one of the most misunderstood members of society. He never blamed people for the disconnect. He accepted that the gap between his day-to-day activities and theirs was too wide to comprehend easily. While he spent his days thinking about stuff, the rest of the world woke to an alarm clock, got the kids off to school, and worked for forty hours per week. Plato wrote *The Allegory of the Cave* to bridge this gap by using a fictional story to help them understand the joys and frustrations of being a philosopher.

The *Allegory of the Cave* described a group of people who lived their entire lives chained to a cave wall. Since their fixed positions didn't allow a line-of-sight view through the cave's entrance, they observed the shadows of things that passed by instead. Therefore, rather than seeing life, the occupants only saw a distorted representation of it.

Then one day, a captive escaped his chains to see the world's grandeur for the first time. He discovered a familiar yet alien world. While shadows allowed the cave dwellers to see the shape of an object, the escapee couldn't have imagined two additional properties: color and dimension. Excited about his discovery, the former captive returned to the cave to share his experiences, but soon realized his handicap. He had no common vocabulary to describe color or dimension. To his chained friends, he spoke gibberish.

The story of my life, Cade thought. He knew exactly what it felt like to describe colors and dimensions to people who'd seen neither. But, that's the job he chose. If he was going to excel in this field, he'd need to act more like Plato and find creative ways to explain things from the everyday perspective instead of his own.

Plato wasn't the only Greek who taught lessons through contrived situations. More than a century before Plato's allegories, Aesop taught morality through fables. Like allegories, fables used contrived situations, frequently relying on anthropomorphism as the backbone to stories such as *The Tortoise and the Hare*, *The Lion and the Mouse*, or *The Wolf in Sheep's Clothing*.

Cade then remembered one more ancient teacher-storyteller. Just as Plato taught philosophy through allegories and Aesop taught morality through fables, the rabbi, Jesus of Nazareth, taught faith through parables.

The components of wisdom-transfer were right

in front of him. Fables, allegories, and parables were all didactic narrative forms designed to teach. All three had successfully passed their wisdom from generation to generation for over two millennia. *Aesop's Fables* were over twenty-five hundred years old; *The Allegory of the Cave* was over twenty-three hundred years old; and the relative newcomers, parables, like *The Prodigal Son*, *The Good Samaritan*, and *The Parable of the Mustard Seed*, were still over two thousand years old. Something about these wisdom-delivery mechanisms made them resilient to the ravages of time.

Yet, for all their strengths, fables, allegories, and parables shared two weaknesses. First, they required many pages to transfer their wisdom—a major issue when considering the sea of information that people swim in every day. Second, they required extraordinary skills to create: the imagination of a storyteller, the dedication of a writer, and the astute capabilities of an editor.

The more Cade thought about it, fables, allegories, and parables were like wisdom shadows on his own cave walls. While they held traits for passing along wisdom, they weren't available to all. Millions of people throughout history had come and gone without ever hearing a fable, allegory, or parable, yet wisdom-transfer occurred nonetheless.

There had to be a more efficient way to transfer wisdom. He just needed to find it.

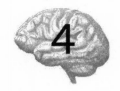

Function Words

Mighty oaks from tiny acorns grow

Sam replayed something that Tina had told her in the limo. *Short, sweet and to the point. The ultimate long-story-short.* She'd always admired people who could express themselves succinctly. While long, flowery descriptions were nice sometimes, her nerd-side preferred people who'd just cut to the chase. "So, how do you build the ultimate long-story-short?" Sam asked.

"It all starts with the words," Tina said. "We need to find out if proverbs use words differently than other linguistic forms."

"And how do we do that?"

"We start with a baseline, like the top ten most used words in the English language." She turned her screen toward Sam to reveal an ordered list.

1. the
2. be
3. to
4. of
5. and
6. a
7. in
8. that
9. have
10. I

Tina continued. "These ten words represent the most popular *function words* that tie all of our sentences together. Although there are only about five hundred function words in the English language, they make up about fifty percent of the words that we use every day."

"They're so common," Sam said. "And little. I've never given them much thought."

"Nobody does, but they play a vital role in effective communication. Simple function word choices can change the entire meaning of a sentence. Take the following excerpt from the end of Abraham Lincoln's Gettysburg Address where he describes a "...government *of* the people, *by* the people, and *for* the people...""

Of course Sam had heard this phrase many times, but this time was different. She paid attention to the function words: *of*, *by*, and *for*.

"Notice how President Lincoln repeats *people* three times yet changes the function word before each one. *Of the people*, describes the government's origin; *by the people* establishes who's in charge, and *for the people* alludes to whom the government serves."

Sam marveled at how three, tiny words could have so much impact. "So, I'm guessing that proverbs use different function words?"

"Believe it or not, they're virtually identical. A word-frequency analysis shows that Mr. Kemper's list shares eight of the top ten commonly used English words."

Sam sounded disappointed. "They do?"

"They do, but there's something to be learned from the areas of non-overlap. The tenth most used word in the English language, *I*, is virtually absent from proverbs."

Sam recalled the morning's example proverbs and wondered if any used the word *I*?

Tina anticipated her question. "Of Mr. Kemper's proverbs, the word *I* only shows up twice…"

"Really? Sam interrupted.

"…and both instances reside in the same proverb, *Do as I say, not as I do.*"

"If the word *I* is one of the top ten most used words in the English language, why is it essentially void within proverbs?"

"It gave me a theory to follow. To find out, I ran Mr. Kemper's proverbs through LIWC."

"What's a Liwwick?" Sam mimicked Tina phonetically.

Tina laughed. "Sorry. It's an acronym that stands for Linguistic Inquiry and Word Count—a text analysis tool developed by function word expert, James Pennebaker. Pennebaker's research reveals how our function word choices say more about us than we might think. He's shown how they reveal psychological states, how we self-assess our status socially, and in some extreme cases, can even determine our truthfulness."

"Now I'm really interested in function words," Sam said.

"LIWC reads through text, removes everything except function words, and then categorizes them."

"What sort of categories?"

"Adjectives like *free*, *happy*, *long*; articles like *a*, *an*, *the*; and negative emotions like *hurt*, *ugly*, *nasty*."

"How many LIWC categories are there?

"Eighty-one." [5]

"And what did you find?"

"When I compared the LIWC results of Mr. Kemper's proverbs with those from forty-nine other literary works[6], like *A Tale of Two Cities*, *Frankenstein*, *Little Red Riding Hood*, or the *US Constitution*, proverbs rank first in twenty-one percent of the LIWC categories."

"First?"

Tina tapped her screen a few times. "Look at this. Compared with forty-nine other literary works, proverb function words rank in the top ten of these LIWC categories:

---

[5] While the LIWC analysis reports calculations for 81 categories, only 72 were used in Tina's analysis. Refer to the back-matter for the categories used.

[6] See back-matter for list of the works used

Rank	Category
1	**Achievement** (win, success, better)
1	**Affective Processes** (happy, cried)
1	**Articles** (a, an, the)
1	**Biological Processes** (eat, blood, pain)
1	**Certainty** (always, never)
1	**Common Adjectives** (free, happy, long)
1	**Comparisons** (greater, best, after)
1	**Health** (clinic, flu, pill)
1	**Money** (audit, cash, owe)
1	**Negations** (no, not, never)
1	**Negative Emotion** (hurt, ugly, nasty)
1	**Positive Emotion** (love, nice, sweet)
1	**Reward** (take, prize, benefit)
1	**Risk** (danger, doubt)
2	**Auxiliary** Verbs (am, will, have)
2	**Present Focus** (today, is, now)
3	**Drives**
3	**Feel** (feels, touch)
3	**Ingestion** (dish, eat, pizza)
3	**Sadness** (crying, grief, sad)
4	**2nd person** (you, your, thou)
4	**Friends** (buddy, neighbor)
4	**Motion** (arrive, car, go)
5	**Body** (cheek, hands, spit)
5	**Death** (bury, coffin, kill)
6	**Differentiation** (hasn't but, else)
6	**Time**

7	**Anger** (hate, kill, annoyed)
8	**Common Verbs** (eat, come, carry)
8	**Quantifiers** (few, many, much)
9	**Cognitive Processes** (cause, know, ought)
9	**Emotional** Tone
10	**LIWC Dictionary Words**

"Do you see any patterns?" Tina asked.

Sam studied the list but nothing jumped out immediately. "I don't know. Perhaps something to do with emotions?"

"Close. Proverbs use function words that describe the human condition. The results blew my mind because they validated another one of Mr. Kemper's theories." She fanned through Mr. Kemper's notebook. "Listen to this. *Proverbs cover five areas of the human condition: feelings, health, achievement, motivations, and relationships.*"

"Okay, since proverbs offer words to live by, it makes sense that they'd lead in those function word categories. But what about the function words that proverbs don't use, like the word, *I*? What categories do proverbs rank last?"

"Let's take a look," Tina said. "Here are the seventeen function word categories where proverbs rank in the bottom ten."

Rank	Title
41	**Female References** (girl, her, mom)
42	**1st Person Plural** (we, us, our)
43	**Assent** (agree, OK, yes)
43	**Space** (down, in, thin)
44	**Sexual** (horny, love, incest)
45	**1st Person Singular** (I, me, mine)
45	**3rd Person Singular** (she, her, him)
45	**Words > 6 letters**
46	**1st Person Singular** (I, me, mine)
46	**Total Function Words** (it, to, no, very...)
47	**Personal Pronouns** (I, them, her)
47	**Total Pronouns** (I, them, itself)
48	**Words Per Sentence**
49	**Conjunctions** (and, but, whereas)
49	**Past Focus** (ago, did, talked)
49	**Prepositions** (to, with, above)
49	**3rd Person Plural** (they)

Sam pointed to first person singular (I, me, mine) at 46th. "That's consistent with what we learned earlier."

"*We* and *they* are also in the bottom ten."

"Wait. Proverbs don't use first or third-person pronouns?"

"Neither in singular nor plural forms," Tina said.

She scrolled backward to reveal the top ten again. "Now look at this."

Sam saw it immediately. Second person pronouns like *you*, *your*, and *thou* ranked 4th. "That's interesting. Proverbs use the word *you* in high frequencies and almost never use the word *I*. Does that fact support Mr. Kemper's Benefit Rule?"

"James Pennebaker would probably agree. He says that our choice of personal pronouns reveals where we see ourselves socially. He found that ...*the person who uses more second-person pronouns like you and your is likely to be the person higher in (social) status.*[7] He also found that the opposite is true. *People who use the word I at high rates are focusing on themselves.*[8] Therefore, if proverbs are indeed wise old sayings that pass life lessons from generation to generation, it's natural to assume that proverb speakers would be older, wiser, and more experienced than proverb listeners, thus leading to their choice of the word *you*."

"My coworker Justin uses the word *I* all the time. Everything's about him. He's always talking about *his* ideas, *his* accomplishments, and *his* experiences."

---

[7] James W. Pennebaker, Secret Lives of Pronouns (New York: Bloomsbury Press, 2013), Kindle e-book location: 2673/5369.
[8] Pennebaker: 2679/5369.

Tina nodded. "Over the years I've come to believe that people who use the word *you* in high frequencies have enough self-confidence to focus their attention on others instead of themselves."

Sam wondered about her own word choices. Which ones did she choose when presenting her ideas? "So, if I want to be more effective in my communications, I need to use the word *you* more?"

"And combine it with the urgency of the present."

Sam blinked. Just when she thought that she was beginning to understand proverbs, Tina threw her a curve ball. "The urgency of the present?"

"Expressing your idea with the word *you* is a powerful way to establish credibility. Choosing the appropriate verb tense multiplies that power." Tina slid her screen closer. "Take another look at the top and bottom LIWC tables. Proverbs rank 2nd in *present focus* and 49th in *past focus.*"

Sam put the two ideas together. "So, proverbs are predominantly written in the second person, present tense?"

"That's the academic way to look at it. I prefer to say that proverbs are about *you* and *now*. And there's one more thing to consider. While the third-most used word in proverbs is *is*, it doesn't even crack the top 100 of the most commonly used words in the

English language."

"So, there must be something special about the word *is*."

"I agree."

A voice came over the cabin's loudspeaker. "Ladies and gentlemen, in preparation for our landing, please return to your seats, put your seat backs up and place your tray tables into their upright and locked positions. We'll be coming through the cabin in a few minutes to pick up any remaining items."

"I forgot to ask," Tina said. "Where are you off to?"

"Boston," Sam said.

"Really? Where do you live?"

"Westford."

"I live in Andover."

"Awesome! Are you on the 5:45 flight to Logan?"

"No, I'm not going directly home. I'm staying in Chicago to give another keynote."

"Oh," Sam said disappointedly.

"Don't worry, Sam. I'm not done with you yet. You have lots of homework to do. Here's my card.

Send me an email."

THE COFFEE SHOP bustled with activity. Glassy-eyed patrons ordered their favorite caffeinated beverages: espressos, mocha lattes, or just regular cups o' Joe.

"Mornin,' Americano," the pretty barista said with a big smile. "The usual?"

"Yes, please," he said. "Thanks, Jenn."

Cade found a table and observed the diversity of the coffee shop's clientele. Anxious sales reps awaited clients, information workers tapped on their keyboards, while the rest stared into oblivion until their recently consumed caffeine snapped them out of their zombie-like states. Cade saw them all as modern-day cave-dwellers reacting to the illusions of their individual cave walls.

Illusions, Cade thought. An illusion can't transfer wisdom because it distorts the facts, but its homophone, *allusion* can. Allusions convey meaning through cultural references. For example, someone who questioned a weak argument may reference an old hamburger commercial by asking, *"Where's the Beef?"* Or, someone trying to describe a complex situation might allude to Dorothy in the Wizard of Oz by saying, *"We're not in Kansas anymore."*

Could allusions be the short narrative form that he was looking for? They, like fables, allegories, and parables conveyed meaning through building upon prior knowledge, but that's where the similarities diverged. Long story-forms drew their strength from shared human experiences. Allusions, on the other hand, were built upon specialized knowledge. Anyone with life experience can draw from the long-form works, but only a subset can extrapolate the nuanced wisdom contained in allusions.

So, allusions were out. Cade needed something more universal to convey wisdom—something with the robustness of fables, allegories, and parables, yet the compactness of allusions.

"Americano?" Jenn called from behind the counter. She looked around the café to see Cade in his typical state—staring off into space. "Cade!" she shouted a few decibels louder than before. He didn't budge. Rather than calling out for a third time and disturbing the other patrons, she walked over. "Yoo-hoo?" she said, tapping him on the shoulder."

Cade flinched. "Oh, sorry, Jenn. I was just working on something."

"You seem to do that a lot." Jenn had been trying to get Cade's attention for a few months. He came in every day, ordered a large Americano, then proceeded to stare into the parking lot for hours at a time. At first, she thought he was just shy, however, when he wasn't in his vegetative state, he'd talk to anyone who'd listen. A coworker mentioned that he was a professor or something. "So, where's your girlfriend this morning?" she probed transparently.

That snapped him out of his thought-induced trance. "Girlfriend?" he blurted. "Oh, you mean Sam? She's not my girlfriend. Just a close friend."

"Really? How close?" Jenn pried.

Before he could answer, Jenn's boss interrupted their conversation. "C'mon, Jenn!" He tapped his watch. "Time is money."

Jenn rolled her eyes. "Okay, I'm coming." She looked back to continue her inquisition but noticed a change in Cade's gaze. Rather than looking at her, he appeared to be looking through her.

"Time is money," Cade mumbled.

"I know. Lame, right?"

"It's a metaphor."

"It's a what?"

"Jenn!" The manager roared.

"I said, I'm coming!"

Cade grabbed his jacket and bolted toward the door. "Sorry, Jenn, but your boss just gave me an idea."

"Wait!" she said waving his freshly brewed cup of coffee. "Aren't you forgetting something?"

Cade never heard her. All he could think of was metaphor. He repeated the phrase over and over until he got to his office where he opened his notebook and found what he was looking for. *Metaphor is principally a way of conceiving of one thing in terms of another, and its primary function is understanding.*[9]

Cade had been attacking the problem in the wrong way. Instead of trying to swallow the wisdom-elephant whole, he needed to do so one bite at a time. *Time is money* helped him break the process of wisdom-transfer into two stages. Before one can teach, one must first learn because metaphor plays a fundamental role in our ability to make sense of everyday experiences. Our...*human thought processes are largely metaphorical.*[10] *Metaphors as linguistic expressions are possible precisely because there are metaphors in a person's*

---

[9] George Lakoff and Mark Johnson, Metaphors We Live By (University of Chicago Press, 2003), Kindle e-book location 625/4362.
[10] Lakoff and Johnson 142/4362.

conceptual system.[11]

Jenn's manager didn't mean that time was literally money. He meant it figuratively—a way of understanding one form of measurement through another. Human experiences teach us that everything carries a cost. Since both time and money are both scarce resources, people assign value to them. Jenn's budget-conscious manager equated every idle minute as a drain on his budget, thus every moment Jenn spent flirting with Cade was costing him money.

Cade finally had a new way of looking at wisdom and its transfer. Before, he saw it as a top-down methodology, delivered through long story-form devices. But, now he saw it as more of a bottom-up device. Every allegory, fable, parable and even allusion was built upon some foundational knowledge. Could that foundation be built upon metaphor? He felt as if he had broken the bonds of his own cave walls to see his problem in spectacular three-dimensional technicolor. Metaphor served as a link between learning and teaching and as a bonus, it came disguised as a short-form narrative.

Cade reached across his desk for a non-existent

---

[11] Lakoff and Johnson 142/4362.

object. "Hey," he said to his empty office. "Where's my coffee?

SAM'S CONNECTING FLIGHT to Boston was just the way she liked…uneventful. She sat next to a perfect seatmate who offered a pre-flight "Hi," read his book for the entire flight, and said "Bye," while deplaning.

Plane flights offered Sam quiet times to think, so she recounted her last presentation—the one mercifully saved by a hardware malfunction. No matter how much time she spent preparing, she just couldn't hold her audience's attention the way that Justin did. But the more she thought about it, the more she saw how Justin had the opposite problem. While he used wit and humor to hold people's attention, his audiences rarely remembered anything that he said. Sam concluded that they were both bad presenters. She had the facts; he had the stage presence, yet neither could leave the audience smarter than they found them.

Well, until now.

Sam had just acquired a secret weapon. She began typing notes into her tablet.

Proverbs contain the who, what, why, when, where and how of information…all in less than 129 characters.

Who? *You*
What? *The topic of the proverb*
Why? *To convey wisdom*
When? *Now*
Where? *Here*
How? *Through using the right function words*

She pressed her nose to the glass to observe the plane's ominous descent toward Boston harbor. Just as it felt as if the plane's landing gear would hit the water, terra firma appeared, the tires squealed on the tarmac, the engines whined, and the big bird began its turn toward the terminals.

Samantha Kim was home.

The Metaphor

It is what it is

Cade reviewed his progress with the Advisor. He discussed four different ways to convey wisdom: fable, allegory, parable, and allusion. And then he described his most recent dive into metaphor. "George Lakoff and Mark Johnson have done some great work on metaphors and how they tie into our ability to understand things," he said. "Metaphor plays an extensive role...*in the way we function, the way we conceptualize our experience, and the way we speak.*[12] Humans build knowledge upon our experiences and explain them through metaphor."

"What do you mean?"

Cade read an excerpt from his notes. *...metaphor pervades our normal conceptual system. Because so many of*

---

[12] Lakoff and Johnson 1946/4362.

the concepts that are important to us are either abstract or not clearly delineated in our experience (the emotions, ideas, time, etc.) we need to get a grasp on them by means of other concepts that we understand in clearer terms (spatial orientations, objects, etc.). This need leads to metaphorical definition in our conceptual system.[13] We are physical beings, bounded and set off from the rest of the world by the surface of our skins, and we experience the rest of the world as outside us. Each of us is a container, with a bounding surface and an in-out orientation. We project our own in-out orientation onto other physical objects that are bounded by surfaces. Thus, we also view them as a container with an inside and outside.[14] Put another way, people have shared experiences. We use metaphor to explain them to ourselves first, then we use both long and short-form narratives to explain those ideas to others."*

The Advisor leaned back in her chair. "Okay. Define shared experiences."

"We experience life through our many senses, like sight, sound, smell, taste, and touch. We learn to interpret these sensory experiences into meaning. At some early point in our lives, we realize that we're separate entities from the rest of the world, which helps us understand the concept of boundaries—

---

[13] Lakoff and Johnson 1946/4362.

[14] Lakoff and Johnson 521/4362.

that our bodies have insides and outsides and those bodies can be inside and outside other containers. This universal human experience leads to the incredibly complex concept that we're all separate beings, which forms one of the most fundamental building blocks for sharing even more complex concepts."

"How so?"

Cade flipped through his notebook. "Take our internal sense of orientation for example. *Since people typically function in the upright position, see and move forward, spend most of their time performing actions, and view themselves as being basically good, we have a basis in our experience for viewing ourselves as more up than down, more front than back, more active than passive, more good than bad. Since we are where we are and exist in the present, we conceive of ourselves as being here rather than there, and now rather than then.*[15] "

Cade's progress pleased the Advisor. Not only had he kept his promise by remaining on topic, but he'd narrowed it too. This deep-dive into metaphor seemed more coherent than his emotional ramblings about portable media devices. "So, if metaphor is *principally a way of conceiving of one thing in terms of*

---

[15] Lakoff and Johnson 2231/4362.

another," she asked, "how do we use them to convey wisdom?"

"In two different ways. First, metaphors help us learn by bootstrapping our understanding of the complex concepts. Then we share those new concepts through linguistic devices."

The Advisor created an awkward moment of silence by staring off into space. Cade wondered how often he did the same thing. "So," she said, "what's the connection between metaphors and your long story-forms?

"That's the part that I'm working on. I just wanted to get your thoughts before I went down that potential rabbit hole."

"It's worth a little digging. Hopefully, the answer is just below the surface, because while you're obviously making progress, you're still running out of time.

WHILE A WEEK away from the office had its perks, returning wasn't one of them. Sam looked at her screen, took a deep breath, and plowed through her neglected email inbox. She reviewed project schedules, budget spreadsheets, and read competitive analyses. Before too long, each email blended into a dizzying jumble of words and numbers. Thankfully, an inbox-anomaly snapped Sam out of her kaleidoscope-eyed trance.

From: Tina Jowett
To: Samantha Kim
Subject: Your Homework

Hi Sam,

Now that you understand proverbs and the words used to construct them, it's time to dig deeper. Here's a scanned copy of Mr. Kemper's Notebook.

T~

Sam hovered her cursor above the attachment. Should she or shouldn't she? Every fiber in her body wanted to open it, but she resisted the urge. A door-knock interrupted her dilemma.

"Look at that," Justin said. "She's back from her boondoggle."

Sam forced a fake smile. "What can I do for you, Justin?"

He feigned a hurt expression. "What? Can't a co-worker just stop by to say, Hi?"

"Anyone but you, Justin. What do you want?"

"Well, since you brought it up, I need

VendorLine's CP report."

"I thought so," she said, re-burying her nose into her monitor in hopes that he'd go away. "I'll get to it after I climb out from under this pile of emails." Her ploy didn't work. She could still see him through her peripheral vision. "Is there anything else?" she asked without looking up.

"Yeah. We need to talk. A lot has happened since your trip."

"Sounds serious."

"It is. Wanna catch up over lunch?"

Primal instinct told her to decline his invitation, but experience advised otherwise. For all his character flaws, Justin had a remarkable connection with the company's grapevine. The little voice inside her head offered proverbial advice. *Keep your friends close and your enemies closer.*

"Okay," she said. "Noon in the cafeteria?"

"Sure, but Ryan's on my back. I need the VendorLine report by the end of the day."

"But that's ten thousand lines of data!" Sam protested.

Justin shrugged. "Sometimes you just need to take one for the team, Sam."

"HOW'S THE SHOPPING GOING?" Tina asked her literary agent.

"We've got a problem," Kavya said. "The publishers are worried about the book's marketability since it only covers English proverbs."

"That's silly. Proverbs apply to all humans, not just English-speaking ones."

"I tried that argument, Tina. But without examples, it's falling on deaf ears."

Tina saw both sides of the argument. On one hand, equivalent proverbs existed in other languages. The French proverb *C'est la vie*, for example, translated well into the English, *That's life*. But, she also understood the skepticism. Her analysis only covered English proverbs and while her gut felt that the power of proverbs applied universally across all languages, she didn't have the proof. To overcome the skeptics, she'd need to widen her research beyond western languages. "Okay," she said. "Lemme work on it."

SAM SCANNED THE sea of cafeteria tables until Justin's waving arm caught her attention. She paused, reminded herself why she had agreed to this, and sat down.

"Have I told you how stunning you look today?" Justin said as she placed her tray down.

"Thank you," she replied coolly.

"This is nice," he said. "Next time we should try dinner."

"Lunch is just fine, Justin. So, what's up?"

Justin looked for anyone within earshot before beginning to speak in hushed tones. "It's not general knowledge yet, but we lost Pentameter."

The news caught Sam off guard. "What do you mean lost?"

"They fired us."

"That's terrible news, Justin."

"It's worse. They went with Zenekas."

"Zenekas? Craig must have lost it."

"Let's just say that he's hunting for heads to roll."

"Wait," Sam said. "I just got this cryptic meeting invite. Is this the topic of tomorrow's manager's meeting?"

Justin answered with a nod. "That would be the one."

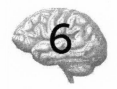

The Present

One today is worth two tomorrows

Grigsby responded to Cade's door knock with the sounds of a ferocious guard dog. The bloodthirsty barks and growls were convincing enough to deter anyone who didn't know any better. Cade knew better.

"Is that all you got?" Cade asked the pug as Sam opened the door. Grigsby's demeanor transformed from fierce to friendly and he jumped into Cade's arms. "Yeah, you're a great watchdog, aren't you?" Cade said, as he carried the pug to the living room, placed his backpack on the floor, and collapsed into Sam's oversized sofa. "How was the trip?" he asked.

"Better than I could have expected. As a matter of fact, I've returned with a gift."

"I love gifts."

Sam handed Cade a glass of wine. "You know

how you're looking for that big secret to human communications?"

"Yeah?"

"I may have found it."

Cade raised his glass. "So, tell me, oh wise one. What is the secret to all human communication?"

"Proverbs," she said, punctuating her statement with a clink of her glass to his.

The quizzical furl of Cade's brow indicated confusion. "Proverbs... umm...like Old Testament stuff?"

"No. Like, finish the following sentence for me stuff. *If at first you don't succeed...*"

"...try, try again," he answered.

"Good. Now, tell me where you learned it."

Cade shook his head. "I have no idea."

"Exactly. That's how proverbs work. We gather them inadvertently through daily experiences, then they lie dormant in our memories until called upon later."

Cade's mind flooded with a thousand questions for Plato, Aristotle, Aesop, and Jesus. "And where did you come up with this epiphany?" he asked.

Sam told him about Tina and Mr. Kemper's Notebook. "Mr. Kemper believed that proverbs were compact communications devices. He called them *the ultimate long-story-short* because proverbs convey more meaning than the words used to construct them. They're short, sweet, and as I just read in his notebook, they pack a meaning-wallop."

Meaning-wallop. Cade appreciated the folksy, yet intellectually-crude description. "*If at first you don't succeed,*" he parsed the phrase out loud, "alludes to some previously failed attempt. *Try, try again,* recommends a way to address that failure." Cade saw how the proverb contained more meaning than its actual words yet didn't understand how exactly. "If you've attempted and failed," Cade continued, "yet still wish for success, you must be prepared to persevere for a second, third, or fourth time." He marveled at how a simple phrase could teach such a complex life lesson: failure is a temporary state that only becomes permanent when you stop trying. "That's amazing, Sam. All that meaning expressed in just nine words."

"Eight," Sam teased. "The word *try* is doubled."

Cade laughed. "And even that little oddity changes the proverb's meaning entirely. Although *try try* is grammatically incorrect, doubling the word prepares the recipient to not only expect continued failure but to persevere nonetheless."

"That's what I like about them," she said. "Not only does every word count, but they also use simple words." She explained Tina's Gunning FOG and LIWC analyses along with Mr. Kemper's Benefit Rule. "Tina believes that the power of proverbs lies in the listener's ability to apply the knowledge immediately." She could see that her last statement got Cade's wheels spinning. It wasn't often that she taught him something, so she celebrated the moment with an extra-large sip of wine.

"That makes sense," Cade said. "The fact that proverbs are applicable to the present situation is likely the reason why they're so effective."

Sam felt her ego dent. Of course, her super-smart friend could rapidly comprehend a concept that she still hadn't fully wrapped her head around. Rather than dwelling in disappointment, she opted to learn why. "Why do you say that?"

"Because people are obsessed with the present. And for good reason. The present can kill you."

"Huh?"

"It's human nature, Sam. The only way to experience the future is to survive this very moment. If proverbs are based in the present, their messages will find fertile ground within human brains that are hyper-focused on both identifying and dealing with present threats. Our brains don't care about the past or the future, only the present. The past isn't a threat, because we've already survived it. And although the future can—and eventually will—kill us, we don't take future threats seriously."

"But, I worry about the future all the time," Sam objected.

"Only if your present situation is secure. Trust me, Sam. If someone held a gun to your head, those future worries would evaporate immediately. It's Maslow's hierarchy of needs. We must satisfy our *physiological* and *safety* needs before anything else, like *belonging and love, esteem, self-actualization,* or *self-transcendence.*[16] We can't care about the future until we're confident that we can survive the present."

It's not that she didn't trust Cade, but she needed to hear it from a second source. She grabbed her tablet to review Tina's LIWC analysis for future tense words and found some contradictory evidence. "I want to believe you, Cade, but what you're saying doesn't line up with Tina's LIWC analysis." She showed him how the frequency of *future focus* function words in proverbs ranked

---

[16] https://en.wikipedia.org/wiki/Maslow%27s_hierarchy_of_needs

twenty-sixth compared with forty-nine other literary works. "So, if our brains don't care about the future, shouldn't future tense words share the bottom with the *past focus* words instead of smack dab in the middle?"

Cade didn't expect to have an argument with Mr. Maslow this evening. "Okay," Cade said. "I wonder if it has something to do with the fact that we care more about the immediate future than the distant future? We flinch at the screech of tires on asphalt because we anticipate an imminent threat." The more he spoke the more convinced he became. "So, let me modify my position. We care about the present, none of the past, and although we care about the near-term future, its relative importance drops off exponentially the farther it's removed from the present. In other words, proverbs focus *predominantly* on the present, *somewhat* on the future, and *never* in the past."

He could see that Sam almost had it.

"Think of it this way," Cade said. "If we truly cared about the distant future, we'd only eat healthy foods, exercise often, and save lots of money for that inevitable rainy day." While Sam wrestled with this information, Cade wondered if proverbs were the missing link between metaphor and long story-forms. "I have a question. Would Mr. Kemper consider the following as proverbs: *justice is blind*; *ignorance is bliss;* and *knowledge is power*?"

Sam tapped her tablet a few times. "Yup. All three are listed in his notebook. Why?"

"I have an idea," Cade said, "but I need to look up something first." The oven timer buzzed as he reached for his backpack.

"We can do that after dinner," Sam said. "Let's eat."

The two friends chatted over dinner as they had hundreds of times before. They talked about work, their personal lives, and the local sports teams. By dessert, the conversation had come back to proverbs.

Since Tina's LIWC analysis showed that proverbs used present tense verbs in high frequency, Cade immediately thought of metaphor. He was particularly interested in the fact that *justice is blind*; *ignorance is bliss;* and *knowledge is power* were both proverbs and metaphors. He wondered if this revelation was the beginning of something interesting or just random coincidence.

He pulled a notebook from his backpack to find something that he'd written down months earlier. It said that...*conventional conceptual metaphor lies at the heart of proverbs...can form the basis of allegory when applied to plot structure…and…the construction of fables.*[17]

And there it was. Metaphor not only *lies at the heart of proverbs*, but it's also the building block for long story-forms. "Sam, I've got to work out a few details, but I think your gift might be the final piece that I need to complete my dissertation."

"Well that sounds like something to raise a glass to," Sam said. "Here's to your latest crazy-ass theory."

Cade shook his head. "Thanks. I think."

BRIGHT SUNSHINE STREAMED through the windows of the Atamaq meeting room in stark contrast to the dark cloud of CEO Craig's presence. Ryan hadn't even closed the door before Craig blurted, "How did Zenekas walk off with our oldest and most loyal customer?" The question hung in the thick air as he surveyed the room for a human to sacrifice.

The present can kill you, Sam thought.

Ryan broke the ice. "Amy said that we've lost our tenacity. Zenekas's project schedules are more

---

[17] Lakoff and Johnson, 4209/4362.

aggressive than ours."

Craig slapped his hand on the table. "That makes no sense!"

"She said that our schedules don't support her customers' needs. While we worked to make our schedules more accurate, Zenekas was recommending ways to shorten them."

Craig continued his interrogation. "Give me an example."

"Zenekas's schedule for Project Shawsheen was half of ours."

"How is that possible?"

"They're willing to take risks."

"And we're not?"

"No. While we invested in traditional ways to optimize delivery schedules, Zenekas developed new technologies."

Craig's face flushed red. "We just survived the largest economic downturn since the Great Depression by being conservative."

"You're right," the VP of Sales chimed in. "But that strategy may have come at a cost. Now that the economy has rebounded, Zenekas has switched to playing offense while we're still playing defense."

Craig seethed. "So, what's your recommendation?"

The VP of Sales looked at the ceiling. The rest of the attendees looked anywhere else to avoid eye contact with their agitated boss. Sam drew doodles in the margin of her notebook.

"…but that's not what a ship is for," she said softly while completing a curly-cue.

All eyes turned to Sam who continued doodling obliviously.

"What did you say, Ms. Kim?" her red-faced CEO asked.

Sam looked up to see all eyes on her. A twinge of dread formed in the pit of her stomach. *Crap!* she thought. *Did I just say that out loud?* Her mind raced for something witty to say.

"Ms. Kim?" CEO Craig repeated.

Sam's answer came out more as a question than a statement. "A ship in the harbor is safe, but that is not what a ship is for?"

The mood of the room chilled as its occupants anticipated an explosion from their volatile CEO. Ryan grimaced; the VP of Sales squeezed his armrest; and Justin silently mouthed the question, "What are you doing?"

"Dammit, she's right!" Craig said to the surprise of everyone in the room. "It's time to put this ship back in the open water. We've weathered the economic storm and it's now time to get back to what we do best. Let's talk ideas."

Nobody spoke, fearing that the first person to speak would get their head bitten off. A few of the managers tested the room with simple ideas until it became clear that Craig wasn't poised for attack. Soon they offered bolder ideas, shared lessons from past projects, discussed risks, rewards, and suggested ways to balance both.

"Great," Craig said. "Let's get to work. Our top priority is regaining Pentameter's trust." He then made a beeline for Sam.

Justin intercepted him before he arrived. "Sir," Justin attempted a thinly veiled attempt at flattery, "I think that your idea is brilliant. I'd like to…"

Craig cut Justin off mid-sentence with his patented don't-mess-with-me stare. "Ms. Kim," Craig said calmly. "Please do me a favor. You have good ideas, but for some reason, you don't express them with enough conviction. In the future, speak up. Okay?"

Sam appreciated the irony of the exchange. Craig expressed his thoughts using the word *you*, both establishing himself as higher in social status while keeping his attention on her. She acknowledged that social status by responding with the word, *I*. "Yes, sir," she said. "I will."

Ryan waited for Craig to leave before approaching. "A ship in the harbor, Sam? Where did that come from?"

"Mr. Kemper's notebook," she said.

"Mr. Who's what?"

"It's a long story."

"HOW GOES THE BATTLE?" the Advisor asked. For the first time, Cade didn't feel defensive because he'd made much progress since the last time they spoke. "I've found a new ally. Paremiology."

"Ah," she said, recognizing the term. "And what have you learned from the study of proverbs?"

Cade reached into his backpack and produced a weathered hardcover book that he'd borrowed from the university's library. He flipped through its yellowed pages and started reading. "Listen to this. *The relation of the fable and the proverb is particularly close...The Aesopic fable, for example, stands godfather to many a proverb...Don't kill the goose that lays the golden eggs; Don't count your chickens before they are hatched…Possibly we have two independent expressions of the same idea, the proverb in the literal and the fable in figurative form.*[18] "

Cade's once jumbled thoughts were starting to fall into place. Metaphor sat at the bottom of a linguistic hierarchy—forming both the foundation of human understanding and the ability to convey that understanding to other people. He'd repeatedly failed to connect that foundation directly to the longer story-forms of allegory, fable, and parable, but he now understood why. He needed a bridge and Sam had built that bridge by introducing him to proverbs.

"I've been trying to make a direct connection between human understanding and the conveyance of wisdom," he said. "I found two different models: short-form conceptual, as in metaphor, and long-form contextual, as in allegory, fable, and parable. The deeper I dive into paremiology, however, the more I see proverbs as hybrid entities that deliver both conceptual understanding and contextualized wisdom."

"Would it be fair to say that you've found a

---

[18] Archer Taylor, The Proverb and an Index to The Proverb (Hatboro: Folklore Associates, 1962), 27-28.

connection between learning and teaching?"

"I would," Cade said. "My friend Sam described proverbs as the ultimate long-story-short," he said, intentionally eliminating the whole *meaning-wallop* part. "But I'm beginning to believe that they're more than that. They're complex linguistic forms that contain premise, conclusion, and a moral of the story." Cade looked directly at the Advisor. "It makes me wonder. Was the proverb, *slow and steady wins the race*, the inspiration for, or the result of Aesop's *The Tortoise and the Hare*?"

"Don't discount the possibility of it being both," the Advisor said. "Perhaps someone asked Aesop if something slow could ever beat something fast. To demonstrate his answer, he invented a plausible way for that to happen—putting a determined turtle into a footrace with an overconfident rabbit." She scribbled a few notes of her own. "I like where this is going, Cade."

"Me too. There's a natural order to it. Proverbs are built upon metaphors while stories are built upon proverbs. Metaphors form the basis for our understanding, while proverbs encode that understanding into mini, thought-inducing messages. Finally, long story forms such as fables, allegories, and parables use story-structure to expand those messages into rich explanations."

"That's a lot of progress since we last spoke."

"Yeah, but now comes the writing."

"Then what are you standing around here for? It's time to get those ideas onto paper."

GRIGSBY GREETED SAM as she came through the front door. It had been a long day. She thought about the manager's meeting, the fact that a proverb had almost gotten her in trouble, and in a weird way, how it also had saved the day. She flipped through her snail mail in hopes of finding anything of value hidden among the leaflets, advertisements, and envelopes. She opened a letter from the property management company to learn of a soon-to-be-started hallway remodeling project.

Sam reached for her tablet. "So, what type of homework do you think Tina sent me this evening?" she asked the pug. Tina's email suggested that Sam read a section of Mr. Kemper's notebook called *Proverbs Make Definitive Statements* on page 88. She found the page and started reading Mr. Kemper's blocky handwriting.

Proverbs Make Definitive Statements

There's nothing wishy-washy about proverbs. They deliver

messages with certainty and strength. Proverbs make bold statements, like:

Love is blind
Successful people are persistent
The first step is always the hardest

The three examples hit home as she recalled Craig's admonition to speak up. She reread the list, this time placing emphasis on the present-tense function words.

Love is blind
Successful people are persistent
The first step is always the hardest

These three examples supported Cade's idea that the human brain cared more about the present than the past or distant future. While definitive statements fed the brain's obsession with real-time events, Mr. Kemper's examples alluded to something deeper. There was something magical about the verb *to be.* Not only did it and its conjugated derivatives *am, is,* and *are* establish a feeling of immediacy, but they came pre-loaded with a second, powerful meaning. Each statement established gravitas—something that eliminated any doubt—which in turn offered a level of comfort for listeners who sought certainty. And while most bold claims drip with arrogance, Mr. Kemper's Benefit Rule allowed speakers to deliver their messages in a paradoxical way: both humbly and with unwavering confidence.

Sam wondered about her own word choices. "Grigsby, do I speak confidently in the present tense, or do I sound wishy-washy by expressing my ideas using *was, can,* or *will be?*"

The pug answered her question with a head tilt.

"When I present charts and graphs, do I speak definitively about the problem at hand, or do I acquiesce into esoteric factoids from the past? When I'm trying to make a point, do I express a concept as an immediate threat, or spend my time lecturing how to solve future problems that may never occur?"

The pooch raised an eyebrow and licked his chops.

"Never mind," she said, before opening her tablet to jot down some notes.

Be more mindful of your vocabulary
Phrase your thoughts in the now
Use the word "is" more

She paused before adding one more line to her

list.

Think in proverbs

Life Policies

Wise it is to comprehend the whole

Cade did his best work outside the confines of his drab office, so he decided to soak in the sun from a park bench. He'd been reflecting on the Advisor's idea that proverbs might act as a connection between learning and teaching. Cade loved teaching. His role as a TA gave him the opportunity to shape young minds and he accepted every opportunity that came his way. He preferred the Socratic method because it allowed him to take an active role in the learning process, where he'd conduct his classroom like an orchestra, posing open-ended questions to tease-out presumptions and prior knowledge. When done correctly, this argumentative form of public dialog helped everyone learn something new—including the teacher.

But, proverbs didn't need an external learning

facilitator. Once a proverb floated from a teacher's mouth to a student's ears, a series of involuntary brain functions extracted, contextualized, and ultimately memorized the wisdom to be recalled at an appropriate time in the future. The process was internal and efficient.

The intensity of the sun's late morning rays forced Cade to seek shade. He followed the sounds of children playing in the distance. As he got closer, he heard frequent bursts of a referee's whistle, but instead of finding a game, he discovered a soccer practice instead.

The coach blew her whistle. "I know that you want to push the ball forward," she told a group of middle school players, "but look at all of the defenders just waiting to collapse on the ball." The players listened, hands on hips while catching their breath. "Now, look behind you," she continued. "See all that open space? Next time, rather than forcing the ball forward into that tight coverage, I want you to pass it back to an open player. *Sometimes it's better to pass the ball backward*," she said.

Cade recognized her proverbish advice instantly. The coach had presented a complex concept through eight simple words. She acknowledged that while the offense's object is to advance the ball and score, the defense's job is to keep that from happening by placing themselves between the ball and the goal. As a result, the closer the offense gets, the more the field of play compresses, which ultimately increases the concentration of defenders and gives them a higher probability of intercepting the ball.

But those eight words also illustrated that the opposite was true. Passing the ball backward not only lowered the risk of getting that pass intercepted, but the move also increased the size of the playing field, which in turn opened more offensive options for advancing the ball. *Sometimes it's better to pass the ball backward.* Cade appreciated the simplicity by which the coach taught such a complex strategy. She didn't need to lead a deep Socratic discussion—her middle schoolers probably wouldn't have listened anyway. She simply broadcasted an encoded message and let the players internalize its meaning individually.

The coach forced the team to practice what she preached. Every time her young players got too impatient and forced the ball into the teeth of the defense, she blew the whistle. "Stop where you are," she said. "Look behind you. See all that open space? I see three players with nobody defending them." She blew the whistle again to reset the cycle, the team dutifully passed the ball backward before falling back into their old habits, when she'd interrupted the pattern again. Soon, the whistles came less frequently as the coach shifted her approach from highlighting mistakes to rewarding their new behaviors with praise. Three whistle bursts signaled the end of practice.

"Okay, huddle up," Cade heard her say. "So, what did we learn today?"

The team droned in unison. "Sometimes it's better to pass the ball backward."

Cade had just witnessed an example of proverbs bridging the gap between teaching and learning. The coach needed a way to convey a non-intuitive strategy to her players, so she bookended her lesson with an identical premise and conclusion. As a premise, the proverb gave the players something to ponder. By the end of the practice, that premise had been tested, proven to work, and thus became a memorized conclusion to be called upon later. The next time an offensive player saw a compressed field with no open area to pass the ball safely, she'd recall the coach's *policy* and pass the ball backward.

Proverbs as policy. Cade had never thought about the word that way. Policy usually accompanied bland subjects like insurance, economics, or foreign relations. But this new definition positioned proverbs as life policies that presented situational rules to live by.

The soccer practice was a metaphor for life. Just as our ancestors passed their wisdom to proliferate the species, the coach passed hers to proliferate the game. Each did so through memorable and repeatable policies that make a life worth living or a game worth playing. Proverbs were rules for a better living, designed to be shared by people who've been-there-done-that to those who will inevitably encounter everyday situations such as success, failure, love, hate, or a gaggle of defenders between an offense and the goal. Proverbs delivered simple rules to help inexperienced people make experienced decisions that if heeded, would ultimately lead to better outcomes.

Cade scribbled some notes.

The journey is the reward
If you don't know who the sucker at the table is, you're it
He who shares proverbs enriches the lives of others

TINA GLANCED AT the number displayed on her buzzing cell phone. "Good morning, Sam," she answered. "How are your studies coming?"

"Let's just say that it's been enlightening. I find

myself constantly thinking in terms of proverbs."

"I should have warned you about that. Occupational hazard," Tina chuckled.

"Hazard is right. You'll never guess what happened yesterday," Sam said, before recounting her contribution to the manager's meeting.

"You didn't."

"I did. Luckily, that old proverb did more good than harm."

"Which probably means that you're ready for your next lesson. Now that you're adding old proverbs to your communications vocabulary, it's time to learn how to construct new ones."

"Sounds great. When do we start?"

"Let's see how far we can get before my next call."

"I'll take whatever I can get, Tina."

"To recap, most proverbs are built upon second-person pronouns (you) and present tense verbs (is/are). Now let's look at some of the ways that proverb authors couple those words. Mr. Kemper spent some time studying bigrams."

Repeating words always helped her memorize better. "Bigrams," Sam said.

"A bigram consists of two words. Do you have

that copy of Mr. Kemper's notebook that I sent?"

"Yes."

"Go to page ninety-six."

Sam did as she was told. "Okay, I'm there." She could see that Mr. Kemper included a list of the top ten bigrams that occurred within his fifteen-hundred proverbs:

Rank	Bi-gram	Occurrences
1	is the	59
2	you can't	50
3	is a	43
4	better to	39
5	if you	38
5	he who	38
6	in the	36
7	of the	35
8	is better	34
9	you can	31
10	it is	29
10	what you	29

"There are many ways to construct proverbs," Tina said. "Mr. Kemper believed that bigrams were as good a place to start as any."

Sam looked at the list and noticed something immediately. "Four of these contain the word, *is*.

"True. And why is that important?" she quizzed her student.

"Besides the fact that it's the basis of the present tense, I just read how the word also makes statements definitive, such as *necessity is the mother of invention; conscience is a soft pillow; and it is always darkest before dawn.*"

"Someone's been doing her homework," Tina said approvingly. "Wisdom must be decisive and unambiguous, which is why proverbs preach what's best and worst as opposed to what's half-hearted or noncommittal."

Sam began feeling comfortable with proverbs. With each day, her brain seemed a little more conditioned to not only accept them but to find ways of incorporating them into her communications. But something bothered her about the fifth bigram, *he who.* "This may sound weird, Tina, but are proverbs misogynistic?"

"It's not a crazy question, Sam. I remember thinking the same thing when I learned about the huge gender disparity in Mr. Kemper's proverbs. For example, the word *he* is found fifty-two times while *she* is only found twice. There are forty instances of *his* compared with one for *her*, sixty-one instances of *man* compared with only five for *woman*." Tina paused to let that sink in. "But this disparity has less to do with misogyny and more to do with a flaw in the English language—the fact that it lacks a gender-neutral singular pronoun. That flaw handicaps our abilities to express a trait or ability in a genderless way. For better or worse, previous generations used the masculine *he/his* when describing a generic person."

Sam thought of her own struggles with the flaw. "I deal with this problem in my report writing," she said. "If I use the word *customer*, I'm eventually forced to choose between *he* or *she* later in the document. I get around the problem by using the plural, *customers*, so that when I eventually need a pronoun later, I can use *they* or *them*."

"It comes down to the intent of the speaker. While the misogynist's intent is to demean, we've already established that the proverb speaker's intent is to pass along wisdom.

"The Benefit Rule," Sam clarified.

"So, when a speaker says *he who* laughs last, laughs best; *he who* rises late must trot all day; or *he who* sings drives away sorrow, the intent is to convey wisdom. And there's one more reason why the bigram works," Tina said. "It's alliterative, thus making it fun to say and easy to recall. Give it a try. Say *he who* ten times and try not to smile. Now, do the same thing for *she who* or *anyone who*. See what I mean? Proverbs are designed for all people, independent of gender. The fact that *he who* is just fun to say is icing on the cake."

A tone at the other end of the line interrupted their conversation. "I hate to do this to you, Sam, but it's the call I've been waiting for. There's lots to learn about bigrams. Are you up for more self-study?"

"I am," Sam said. "Good luck with your call."

"Thanks," Tina said before the line clicked dead.

TINA VIEWED TRAVELLING much differently than her younger self. Back then, jet-setting around the world seemed exciting. Today, however, she saw it as a necessary evil that took valuable time from her family. But, not this evening. Tonight, she looked forward to sharing a table with her parents, husband and two children.

"How's the book coming?" Grandpa Jake asked his daughter.

"Slow," Tina said. "It seems that proverbs are more exciting to talk about than to write about."

"Well," he said with raised eyebrows, "the subject is a little dry. You might..."

"Hey, Grandpa!" six-year-old Bobby interrupted. "Can we play catch after dinner?"

"Bobby," Tina admonished. "It's rude to interrupt people when they're talking."

"I'm sorry, Mommy, but it's getting dark outside."

"Well, only if it's okay with Grandpa…"

"It is," Grandpa Jake said.

"…and after you finish your vegetables," Tina qualified.

"Yuck. I hate brussels sprouts."

"Tell you what," Grandpa Jake said. "Finish 'em up while I get the gloves from the basement. We'll play catch when I come back."

Bobby stared at his grandfather's plate of unfinished brussels sprouts. "How come I have to finish mine but Grandpa doesn't have to finish his?"

Tina resisted the urge to grin. The kid had a point.

"Do as I say, not as I do," Jake said, before heading toward the basement door.

"Hey, Mom," Tina's twelve-year-old daughter Angelee said. "Grandpa Jake just used a *Do/Don't* proverb."

"A *Do/Don't* proverb?" Grandma Sandy asked,

casting a sideways glance at Tina. "Where did you learn that?"

"From Mr. Kemper's notebook. Mom let me read it the other day."

"Really? So, what exactly is a *Do/Don't* proverb?"

Angelee hadn't expected a quiz. "Umm, it's when you tell someone to do something, or not to do something. Right, Mom?"

"Very good. *Do* and *Don't* proverbs recommend actions. For example, when someone with a bad habit is trying to help someone else avoid that same habit, they'll say, *"Do as I say, not as I do."*

"I heard that!" Grandpa Jake called from the basement.

"I can't eat this," Bobby said.

"And when a boy says that he can't do something, his Mom might say something like, "You never know what you can do 'til you try."

"She's right, Bobby!" Grandpa Jake yelled.

"And what about *Don'ts*?" Angelee asked.

"Don't proverbs are special," Tina said. "Mr. Kemper's notebook has twice as many of them than *do proverbs.*"

Bobby bit into a brussels sprout and made a face.

"That's all you and Daddy ever say. 'Don't do this, Bobby, don't do that, Bobby.'"

"We're just trying to protect you. *Don't* proverbs keep people from doing things that aren't good for them."

"Like eating brussels sprouts?" he pushed.

"Like when someone is being over-dramatic, we might say, *Don't cry over spilled milk.*"

"Hey, I got an idea!" Bobby said. "What if I play catch with Grandpa now and finish when we come back in?"

"Then we might say, *Don't put off for tomorrow what you can do today.*"

Grandpa Jake emerged from the basement carrying two gloves and a baseball. "Well? Are you finished, Bobby?"

"Yup! I ate one. That should be enough, right Mommy?" Bobby pleaded.

"And when you know that you can't win an argument," Grandpa Jake said, "someone might say, *Don't try kicking against the wind*, Bobby."

SAM HAD COME a long way since her limo ride to the airport. Tina gave her a solid education in function words, Cade gave her an appreciation for the power of the present, and as a result, she saw proverb potential everywhere she went. But despite this progress, she still lacked a methodological way of creating her own proverbs. No matter how much she learned about function words or metaphors, these revelations were useless without an ability to put them into practice.

But where should she start?

She reviewed Mr. Kemper's list of bigrams for inspiration.

Rank	Bi-gram	Occurrences
1	is the	59
2	you can't	50
3	is a	43
4	better to	39
5	if you	38
5	he who	38
6	in the	36
7	of the	35
8	is better	34
9	you can	31
10	it is	29
10	what you	29

While she recognized their abilities to jumpstart

the creative process, she didn't feel that they were strong enough to build proverbs upon. She needed to find something central—the nucleus of all proverbs. If such a core existed, she'd then have something solid to build her tool upon.

But that's where the task got difficult. How does one find commonality among infinite possibilities? Proverbs covered the alphas and omegas of every subject from friends to enemies, life to death, danger to safety, wisdom to folly, and love to hate. Even Tina's LIWC analysis revealed a cornucopia of function words that ranked first in a mishmash of topics such as: negations (no, not, never), common adjectives (free, happy, long), affective processes (happy, cried), positive emotions (love, nice, sweet), and negative emotions (hurt, ugly, nasty). Sam pressed a palm to her forehead as doubt crept in. She wondered if any common core existed at all.

Perhaps Mr. Kemper had some thoughts on the subject. Page seventeen of his notebook revealed that he did.

The purpose of all proverbs is to evaluate.

Sam related to the statement. Clients hired her to assess situations and make recommendations. But Mr. Kemper didn't stop there. He elaborated by saying that proverbs evaluated three things: *roles, events, and influences.*

Sam grabbed her tablet and started writing. Although she never thought about it before, Sam spent most of her time evaluating roles, events, and influences. Roles were the people, processes, and technologies of her projects. Events were the things that introduced project implications, like when a team member required a leave of absence to care for his aging parents. And lastly, the most critical component of any project, influences identified the motivations behind people's decisions and ultimately provided the best barometer for predicting their actions.

Sam didn't want to get her hopes too high, but this concept showed promise. If evaluation sat at the core of all proverbs and that core could be categorized in three ways, she might have stumbled upon the beginnings of a proverb-making tool. The next question was how?

How did they evaluate? For example, once a proverb creator chose a role, event, or influence to evaluate, what was the next step? The only way for her to answer that question was to slog through all fifteen-hundred of Mr. Kemper's proverbs and categorize each. Sam suddenly felt very tired and her mind flooded with excuses. "Hey," she said to Grigsby, "I've got that early morning meeting tomorrow. We should probably call it a night, right?"

The sleepy pug looked unimpressed. Sam continued scanning the list sloppily until her eyes stopped on one of Mr. Kemper's proverbs.

Sometimes the best polish is elbow grease

Sam had never met Mr. Kemper; he died when she was a little girl. But at that moment, she felt as if he had just hit her with a playful jab. Sam took a deep breath and resigned herself to the fact that it would be a very long night.

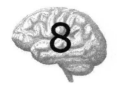

Form & Function

Practice makes perfect

Although it took Sam about three hours to go through all of Mr. Kemper's proverbs, a pattern emerged quickly. She learned that proverbial evaluations were delivered in three different ways: definitions, predictions, and prescriptions.

Definitions came as no surprise considering what Cade had taught her. All proverbs derive from metaphor and thus predominantly carry the word *is*.

Character is destiny

Forewarned is forearmed

A miss is as good as a mile

She particularly liked predictions because they checked all the boxes that appealed to her scientific mind. Since she spent most of her time as a consultant identifying and studying causal relationships, she appreciated a proverb-type dedicated to them.

Haste makes waste
Rats desert a sinking ship
When the wine is in, the wit is out

And finally, prescription proverbs offered advice that either fixed something or kept it from breaking in the first place.

Look before you leap
If you can't beat them join them
When the bait costs more than the fish, it's time to stop fishing

Sam liked her progress. She'd found a method for crafting digestible statements that shared complex thoughts, added predictability to seemingly unpredictable outcomes, and prescribed ways to fix present ills or prevent future ones. Support for her theory came from an unexpected source—a physicist who'd been dead for almost three centuries. Sir Isaac Newton summarized his three laws of motion as proverbs:

1. *A body at rest, stays at rest, while a body in motion stays in motion*
2. *Force equals mass times acceleration*
3. *Every action has an equal and opposite reaction*

Sam tested her new method by categorizing Newton's axioms. She determined that the first and third laws predicted, while his second law defined. She delighted in the notion that Newton used proverbs, but soon recognized a new problem. Sir Isaac had it easy. The laws of nature were universal—just apply the same force to identical objects and both will react identically. The laws of human nature, however, were messier. Put two different people in the same situation and they'll likely choose different actions.

Or would they? Sam thought. If people have free will and thus can choose any outcome, are their actions truly random? She wished that Cade were here because this question was right up his alley. It was too late to call, so she decided to channel him instead. What would Cade say if she asked him this question?

Sam smiled as she imagined the way his brow crinkled while deep in thought. She imagined how he'd likely argue that her question depended upon the situation and the people involved. He'd likely say that if two people shared the same belief system, then their free will choices would most likely be similar—possibly even identical. And therefore, he'd probably conclude that since all humans share both the need to survive and to avoid pain, situations that threatened either would make predicting human actions that much easier.

Curiosity killed the cat
A disaster teaches more than a thousand warnings
When the fox is charming, watch your chickens

Sam felt a wave of enlightenment rush over her. Mr. Kemper believed that proverbs focus on the human condition. Tina's LIWC analysis confirmed that their function words ranked high for the trickiest parts of the human condition: *feelings, health, achievement, motivations, and relationships.* Finally, by coupling both findings with Cade's work on metaphors—the fact that proverbs are life policies that convey complex concepts—Sam saw how proverbs relied upon shared experiences that humans used to define, predict, and prescribe the roles we play, the motivations behind our actions, and the events that ultimately transpired because of them.

Sam wrote the following:

Proverb Types:

- *Definitions*
- *Predictions*
- *Prescriptions*

She loved the simplicity. The next time she found herself needing to share insight, she'd ask herself, "What am I trying to convey: a definition, prediction, or prescription?" The next step was to determine exactly how they did that. What techniques did proverb authors use to convey their wisdom?

Sam looked at the wall clock and yawned. It wouldn't be tonight.

CADE SAW THE SPIDER through the corner of his eye, dashing any hopes of continuing his work until the eight-legged intruder's demise. His heart rate surged as he used one eye to seek a weapon of mass destruction while the other remained locked on the uninvited visitor. The only weapon within reach was a tissue, setting the stage for a daring duel of hand-to-multiple-leg combat.

Now came the tricky part. Cade needed to

position the tissue within a perfect striking distance. Strike from too far away and the creature would have enough time to flee. Get too close and risk triggering the arachnid's spidey sense. Either outcome resulted in an untenable situation—Cade would never be able to work in his office again.

Cade's pulse increased the closer the tissue got to the spider. Every fiber of his being focused on the task at hand as he mentally calculated the optimal striking distance.

Just...a little...closer.

Cade pounced; the spider leaped, but not before being crushed with force of a terrified philosopher. Refusing to leave anything to chance, Cade pinched the tissue between his thumb and forefinger with enough power to squeeze juice from a raisin. A chill ran down his spine as he tossed the tissue coffin into the toilet and flushed.

Had it not been for the smudge that remained at the site of the violent altercation, it would have been a perfect kill. So, although Cade could finally get back to work, he'd have to do so in the presence of spider guts.

Cade concluded that proverbs were life policies, built upon metaphor, which tied them directly into the human ability to understand. The predominant use of the present tense gave them unfettered access to the skittish part of the central nervous system that cared deeply about today, a tad about tomorrow, and nothing about yesterday.

He peered back at the smudge and laughed. He didn't know the source of his arachnophobia but recognized the power that it held over him. Instinctive reactions tend to cause overreactions when more measured ones are warranted. That hairy spider didn't threaten his life—he squashed it with a tissue for crying out loud—so, why couldn't he break the bonds of instinct with a more effective process like reason?

Cade continued to stare at the smudge and noted the similarities between instinct and proverbial wisdom. They both triggered involuntary actions within our minds. Instinct initiated lightweight quick reactions to deal with hyper-present situations, while proverbs initiated heavy slower ones that lead to deeper understanding. That gave him an idea.

While proverbs rely on slow cognitive processes to unpack the wisdom contained within, once implanted into memory, that wisdom could be recalled later without the overhead required to form that original memory. In other words, proverbs train us slowly today so that we can infer quickly tomorrow. Since memory recall is faster than cognitive thought, listeners benefit from the best of both worlds: the speed of instinct with the accuracy of higher cognitive processes.

"Proverbs are anti-instinct devices," Cade said to the smudge, "a way to short-circuit the power that instinct holds over us."

He who fears death lives not

An injury is forgiven better than an injury revenged

It's not the size of the dog in a fight, but the size of the fight in the dog

Cade typed in a vain attempt to keep up with his cascading thoughts. He described the ability of proverbs to reprogram the negative effects of all instinctive reactions.

A terrifying thought interrupted his typing.

He wasn't trying to eliminate all instincts, just the irrational ones. Coming face-to-face with a spider wasn't deserving of one's fear but coming face-to-face with an angry bear was. If proverbs held the power to reprogram gut reactions indiscriminately, that power came with ethical responsibilities because proverbs could also be used to alter healthy instincts.

Rhetoricians have used proverbial language throughout history to push their agendas. Winston

Churchill...was well aware of the importance of imagery, metaphor, pithiness, idiom, colloquialism, antithesis, and epigram in his speaking and writing.[19]*...Churchill's own inclination towards coining 'proverb-like' phrases did not prevent him from making use of traditional proverbs whenever they suited his rhetorical purposes...He...delighted in using "Deeds, not words" as a leitmotiv 15 times throughout his long life.*[20]

But Churchill wasn't the only World War II figure to underscore his ideas proverbially. Adolph Hitler also used proverbial-laced rhetoric to rally his nation and allies. *The six volumes of (Churchill's) The Second World War contain 410 proverbial texts on a total of 4,405 pages, which yields a ratio of one proverbial phrase for every 10.7 pages...Adolf Hitler used about 500 proverbial phrases in a total of 792 pages of Mein Kampf (My Struggle, 1925/26), making this aggressive, polemic, and propagandistic bible of national socialism and anti-Semitism much more "proverbial" and by extension, manipulative authoritarian.*[21]

Manipulative authoritarian, Cade thought. Illusion versus allusion. Instinct is based on fear and

---

[19] Wolfgang Mieder, Proverbs: A Handbook (Greenwood Press, 2004), Kindle e-book location: 2766/3808.

[20] Mieder: 2829/3088.

[21] Mieder: 2769/3808.

proverbs are based on wisdom. If someone used proverbs to stoke that fear with illusion, a bad actor could undermine the fundamental beliefs that have served civilization well—and lead to evil deeds—such as the extermination of six million innocent people.

RYAN'S CRYPTIC TEXT message instructed Sam to drop what she was doing and come immediately to Craig's office. She walked briskly because one doesn't dawdle when called to the principal's office.

"They're expecting you," Craig's admin said. "Go right in."

Sam had only visited Craig's office once before. On that occasion, she waited alone while he signed a contract. This time, they were joined by two other people: Ryan and Pentameter's CEO, Amy Tennet.

"Thank you for coming, Ms. Kim," Craig said. "You know Amy, right?"

Sam reached out to shake Amy's hand. "Yes, of course," she said.

"I've just spent the past hour groveling for Amy to take us back," Craig said. "It must have worked because she's requesting our help."

Ryan flashed Sam an *I'll explain later* look.

"I'm glad to help. So, what's the problem?"

"Santiago is in trouble," Craig said, trying unsuccessfully to suppress a grin. Sam recognized the name of the project that Zenekas claimed it could complete in half the time that Atamaq did.

"Zenekas promised to deliver the project in six months," Amy said. "They're five months in and are spinning their wheels. They've already punted on two major milestones and evidently have no ability to forecast an end date." She continued to explain that with no viable completion date in sight, Pentameter's end-customer was threatening to sue. Amy needed options. "So that's when I thought of our good friends over at Atamaq."

"And we are so glad that you did," Craig said. "I'm sure that we can get your project back on track, can't we, Ms. Kim?"

"Well, I won't know until I look at the specifics," she said cautiously.

Amy handed Sam a thumb drive. "Everything you need should be right here. If not, here's my cell number. Please call me day or night."

Craig opened his mouth. "We'll get back to you..."

"...in a few days," Ryan said, simultaneously

saving Sam from unnecessary pressure and Craig from a possible need to backtrack later.

"…in a few days," Craig repeated. "Will that work for you, Amy?"

Although Amy would have preferred an estimate in hours not days, she understood. *"Sooner is better than later."*

SAM HAD HIT a brick wall in her quest to understand how to write proverbs, so she had reached out to Tina for help. "There's the Calvary," Sam said as she answered her phone. "Thanks for calling me back, Tina."

"I just listened to your message. It sounds like you're making progress with your proverb construction project."

"I have," Sam said, explaining about definitions, predictions, and prescriptions, "but now that I've defined proverbs by type, I'm stuck trying to figure out precisely how they're written."

Tina instinctively wanted to start with function words, but she felt that Sam was asking a higher-level question. "So, rather than looking at the individual building blocks, you'd like to know how those blocks are assembled?"

"Exactly."

"Okay. Have you thought about the traits that proverbs share with other literary devices like fiction, nonfiction, and essays?"

"No, I haven't, but since we're on that track, let's not forget allegory, fables, and parables," Sam added.

"Cade would be disappointed if we did," Tina chuckled. "So, I'm wondering, what do all of these devices share? What do they all have in common?" The two women let the question simmer for a moment before Tina broke the silence. "What about form and function?"

Form and function, Sam thought. "If they all share form and function, then I might be halfway there. Up until this moment, I've been calling definitions, predictions, and prescriptions proverb types. Now, it feels more accurate to call them *functions* instead. So, if a proverb's *function* is to convey messages through definitions, predictions, and prescriptions, I guess my next step to review each proverb for *form*." Sam experienced a temporary moment of dread as she contemplated another proverb-by-proverb slog through Mr. Kemper's list. The good news is that her call to Tina was successful. The bad news was that she'd be staring at her computer screen for yet another long evening. "Thanks, Tina. I knew you were the right person to call."

"Glad to help. Please keep me updated. I wanna see this new tool of yours in action."

"GOOD MORNIN', AMERICANO," Jenn said in a sing-song voice as she delivered Cade's namesake order. "Yours'll be right up, Sam."

Sam waited for the pretty barista to get out of earshot before mimicking her sing-song voice. "And who's that, Americano?"

"Oh, that's just Jenn."

"Just Jenn, huh? Just Jenn likes you."

"No, she doesn't," he snapped.

"And by that adorable shade of red on your cheeks, I see that the feeling's mutual."

"Remember how those three proverbs: *justice is blind; ignorance is bliss; and knowledge is power* are both proverbs and metaphors?" Cade asked, changing the topic adeptly.

"Yeah?"

"Metaphors describe one thing in terms of something totally different. When we say, *justice is blind; ignorance is bliss; and knowledge is power*, we're using the power of metaphor to encode deep meaning that listeners can decode by using the master key of shared human experiences. *Their brevity holds the secret to human understanding.*[22] "

"'Master key of shared human experience? Really, Cade? Where do you get this stuff?"

Cade laughed. "Take the metaphor/proverb *the journey is the reward.* We've all been on journeys, right?"

Sam nodded.

"Well, our most memorable journeys have unexpected detours, like that time when we ran out of gas in Pittsburgh."

"That wasn't my fault," Sam protested.

"But we laugh about it today. We didn't intend to run out of gas, yet my favorite memories from that trip involve the comedy of errors that ensued because of it. *The journey is the reward* is built upon a shared human experience. No matter where people are from or what language they speak, when a human hears *the journey is the reward* in their native language, they just get it."

"I've been thinking a lot about how proverbs

---

[22] Lakoff and Johnson: 625/4362.

derive their power from the present tense," Sam said. "The fact that metaphor uses the word *is* liberally, makes sense. But I get the feeling that there's something more complex happening in your examples?"

"What do you mean?"

"Not only does the word *is* connect two different concepts cognitively, but it also acts as a boundary that separates them physically. In *justice is blind, justice* and *blind* are only separated by two little letters."

"That's great metaphorical insight, Sam. It comes from the metaphor, *proximity is power.*[23] The closer something is to us, the stronger its effect on us. The fact that two radically different concepts are only separated physically by a one-syllable word increases their effect on each another, at least from a metaphorical perspective."

Sam let *proximity is power* bounce around her brain for a few moments. "So, let me get this straight. Just as our brains pay more attention to present situations over past and future ones, they also pay more attention to things that are closer to us physically?

"We use metaphors to comprehend complex

---

[23] Lakoff and Johnson: 2204/4362.

concepts. Take the concept of time for instance. Since time exists outside the physical bounds by which we live, it's a difficult concept to understand. However, if we can define temporal events using physical terms, we'll have a new dimension to use for comprehension."

"Okay, Mr. Ph.D. candidate. Wanna rephrase that in language that the rest of us can understand?" Sam joked.

"By describing time as an object, we can give it physical properties. The fact that objects have locations allows us to describe time as a location, such as *behind us* for the past and *ahead of us* for the future." Cade stopped to let that settle in. "See what happened there? Now that time is an object that can be in front or behind us, we've now opened ways to describe how far away it is, such as in the near future or far past. Finally, combining this concept with *proximity is power* helps us see how the closer an event is to us in time, the more influence it has upon us."

Sam nodded. "I gotta admit, I fell in love with the word *is* early in this process."

"It changes the meaning of everything. Consider the following two sentences: *Winter is coming,* and *Winter will come*. Both mean the same thing…"

"…but one feels more ominous."

"It's the power of metaphor. Like time, winter is a complicated concept to grasp. However, by using the metaphor *winter is an object*, we've now ascribed it with the ability to move. *Winter is coming* suggests that winter is moving toward to us and thus is increasing its influence with each moment. *Winter will come*, on the other hand, lacks any sense of inevitability. With no immediate threat of its impending arrival, it's easy to ignore as some esoteric thing in the vague, distant, and thus safe future."

Sam admired Cade's ability to explain the most complex ideas simply, yet she also knew that such brilliance came at a price. While Cade was a master of philosophical discourse, he was also an emotional knucklehead. "So, proximity is power?" she asked.

"Yep."

"And the closer something is to us, the more impact it has on us?"

"You got it," he said.

Sam pointed across the room. "Then, get over there and ask that girl out."

The deftness by which Sam had turned the tables caught him flat-footed. "Nnnooo," he stammered. "I can't."

"Why not?"

"Umm...err...what if she's not interested?"

"Trust me, Cade. This is a slam dunk."

Cade's flush red cheeks suddenly drained of their color.

"Cowboy up," she said. *"Faint heart never won fair lady,* ya know."

SAM AWOKE TO the sound of hammering. At first, she thought it was a bad dream, but as the fog of sleep cleared, she remembered the hallway remodeling memo. She tried to ignore the racket while sleep-walking to her coffee maker.

Last night, she'd finally categorized Mr. Kemper's proverbs by form.

Proverb Forms	
Alliteration	Double-use
Association	Ellipses
Assonance	Negation
Comparisons	None (implied)
Conditionals	Opposites
Consonance	Reversals
Conviction	Rhyme
Derivatives	Rhythm

Sixteen categories were just too many. Sam needed to simplify the list, perhaps through subcategories. She manipulated the words in her mind while sipping her morning brew. That's when the hammering stopped, "Hey, Gerry," she heard one of the construction guys call out. "The framin's done."

"Okay," a distant voice replied. "Gimme a sec and I'll help ya with the drywall." Sam heard the clomp, clomp, clomp of heavy work boots approach. "Looks good. Let's start finishin'."

"Finishin," she said aloud in the local accent before a sudden gestalt interrupted her recategorization task. "Finishin'!" she repeated. *Proverbs are like walls*, she thought. Both are built upon frames and then decorated with finishes. Just as drywall is hung on studs and finished with paint and pictures, proverbs hung their function words on frames and finished them with linguistic styles. Frames add structure while finishes increase memorability and repeatability.

She divided her original sixteen categories into two subcategories, resulting in a much more manageable four frames and twelve finishes.

FRAMES

- Comparisons
- Conditionals
- Derivatives
- None (implied)

FINISHES

- Alliteration
- Association
- Assonance
- Consonance
- Conviction
- Double-use
- Ellipses
- Negation
- Opposites
- Reversals
- Rhyme
- Rhythm

Sam stepped back to review her work. Better, but still too heavy, she thought, so she collapsed the list into four frames and five finishing categories.

FRAMES	FINISHES

FRAMES

1. **Comparisons**
2. **Conditionals**
3. **Derivatives**
4. **None (implied)**

FINISHES

1. **Conviction**
2. **Ellipsis**
3. **Negation**
4. **Poetic**
   - Assonance
   - Consonance
   - Rhyme
   - Rhythm
5. **Wordplay**
   - Association
   - Double-use
   - Opposites
   - Reversals

Finally, Sam had something that looked more like a tool for creating the ultimate long-story-short. All one had to do was answer three simple questions:

1. **What's the function of your proverb?** (definition, prediction, or prescription)

2. **What frame will you build the proverb upon?** (comparisons, conditionals, derivatives, none)

3. **What finishes can you add?** (conviction, ellipsis, negation, poetic, or wordplay)

She grabbed a fistful of colored index cards and created a stack of nineteen: three functions, four frames, and twelve finishes.

Now came the moment of truth. The only way to prove the tool's viability was to find people to test it. Luckily, she knew the right two people to ask.

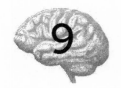

Sam's Cards

A bad workman blames his tools

Sam had spent about a half hour combing through the documents on Amy's thumb drive. She read meeting notes, project documents and studied Gantt charts for any clues to the problem.

Ryan tapped lightly on her office door. "How's it going?"

"I've found a few things, but nothing significant."

"No pressure, but this is a top priority," he said.

"I kinda figured that. Can you give me the rest of the afternoon? I'll have an update by the end of the day, I promise."

"Sure," Ryan said. "Is there anything I can do to help?"

"No. I just need to stare at these documents a little longer."

"I mean in terms of your other work. I need you focused on Pentameter. What can I take off your plate? Justin has some spare cycles."

The corners of Sam's mouth turned upward revealing a wry smile. "Justin? Well, I haven't had a chance to clean up that raw VendorLine data yet," she joked.

"Consider it done," he said before vanishing down the hall.

"Wait!" she called out too late. "I was joking." At first, she felt guilty about tossing her garbage-work to Justin. Then she remembered the countless times that he'd dropped his own messes into her lap. *Turnabout is fair play*, she thought.

Something in the Santiago Gantt caught her eye. Sensor code algorithm development was listed as a one-week effort. She scrolled back to understand the task's impact on the top-level schedule. And there it was, hidden in plain sight. The entire project hung on the completion of Task 83: Sensor Code Algorithm Development.

The sound of angry shoes in the hallway interrupted her thought. "Hey! What did I do to you?" Justin said as he barreled into her office.

"I'm sorry. What?"

"Ryan just gave me your crappy VendorLine work."

"Oh, that. He's just clearing my plate so I can focus on Pentameter."

"But that's millions of raw data records," he protested.

Sam looked up from her screen doe-eyed. "Yes, it is," she said. "Sometimes you just need to take one for the team, Justin."

JENN NOTICED SOMETHING different about the way Cade ordered his coffee. He seemed nervous. "Is everything okay, Americano?"

Cade's heart raced faster than it did during his spider duel. He'd practiced this conversation in his head at least a dozen times, but it just wasn't coming out well. "Yeah...Ah... Well, I..."

Jenn tried to help him. "Hey, I keep forgetting to ask. When you ran out of here last week, how long did it take to realize that you forgot your coffee?"

That made Cade smile. "Oh, about a half-hour," he said sheepishly.

"So, what was that all about, anyway?"

Her question disarmed his anxiety because Cade

could talk with anyone about his work. "You know that thing that your boss yelled out?"

"The *time is money* thing?"

"Yeah. Well, it helped me solve a big problem that I'd been struggling with."

Jenn tried one last time to show her interest. "I'd love to hear more about it sometime."

Cade worried that Jenn could hear his heart beating against his ribcage. "Maybe I could tell you about it over dinner?"

Jenn smiled. "It's about time, Americano. I thought you'd never ask."

SAM KNOCKED ON Ryan's door. "I found something. Whoever built this project plan didn't know much about Pentameter's software development process. The task dependencies are way off."

"Not whoever," Ryan clarified, "It's whatever. Zenekas is experimenting with machine learning for schedule optimization."

Sam had read a few articles about program managers feeding previous project information into machine-learning algorithms. "That might explain it," Sam said.

"Might?"

"The machine may have equated algorithm development with more straightforward programming tasks. I just wrote a simulation model to test a theory. The program's chugging away as we speak, so I should have some results soon."

"Good, because Craig promised Amy that you'd present your findings on Wednesday morning."

Sam's eyes widened. "Wednesday? As in the-day-after-tomorrow Wednesday?"

"Well, you know, Sam, *a ship in the harbor is safe and all*," he joked. "That reminds me, when are you going to tell me that long story about Mr. Krispy's notebook?"

"Kemper."

"Whatever. Spill."

Sam recited a high-level overview of proverbs, the Benefit Rule, Tina's work with function words and Cade's investigation into metaphors.

Ryan laughed. "Sam. When I told you to find your thing, I didn't mean from an old dead guy."

Sam ignored his teasing. "You want to see how proverbs work, or not?"

"As long as I'm not taking you away from Pentameter."

"You aren't. The simulation won't be done for at least an hour. Don't move."

Sam left his office and returned with a stack of colored index cards. She explained to him about how all proverbs evaluated roles, events, and influences, how those evaluations had functions, were built on frames and were decorated with finishes. It took about fifteen minutes for Ryan to grasp the concept, but once he had it, he wanted to know more. He pointed to the *Wordplay: Opposites* card. "What's an opposite?"

"Opposites use irony to deliver meaning through paradox."

"For example?"

"*A bully is always a coward.* By defining an aggressive person as a coward, our minds must rectify the paradoxical nature of the statement. Somehow, that thought process leads us to recognize a fundamental truth of a bully's true motivations."

"Schoolyard bullies overcompensate for their insecurities," Ryan said.

"And it all comes from the power of using

opposites as a proverbial finish. *A broken clock is right twice a day; one man's loss is another man's gain; hope for the best, plan for the worst.*"

"*The best offense is a good defense,*" Ryan added. "I get it, Sam. But, so what? How's this stuff useful?"

Sam raised her eyebrows. "You do remember my last presentation, right?"

"Are you still hung up on that?"

"I spent hours preparing for that presentation yet none of them were dedicated to making it meaningful for my audience. I'm hoping that these index cards will help me both hone and encapsulate my messages into effective delivery mechanisms."

"Since you brought it up, do you have any proverbial wisdom to share with Amy on Wednesday?"

"Nothing yet, but I'm hopeful that I will after wrapping my schedule analysis."

DINNER COULD HAVE gone either way. Such is the risk when introducing two friends. Luckily, Tina and Cade bonded over their mutual obsession with linguistics, spending the entire dinner grokking over function words, metaphor, policy, and some other academic phrases that Sam had never heard of.

"Can I get you anything else?" the waiter asked.

"Coffee for me," Tina said. Sam and Cade followed suit.

"So, how long have you known each other?" Tina asked.

"We met as freshmen in college," Cade said.

"And how long have you been dating?"

Sam almost spit her wine across the table. "You think we're a couple?"

"Oh, sorry. You aren't?" Tina said. "You talk about Cade all the time and you seem so comfortable together. I just assumed."

"Don't get me wrong, I love Sam," Cade said. "Just not in *that* way," he clarified.

"Ditto. Besides," Sam said in her sassy voice, "Cade's got his eye on a certain barista."

"Really?" Tina said. "And does this barista have a name?"

Cade could only take so much of the estrogen-fueled teasing and put an end to it. "So, Sam. You wanted to show us your magical proverb cards?"

"Yes," Tina said. "I can't wait to see how they're coming along."

Leave it to Cade to keep us on task, Sam thought. She pushed her wine glass aside, pulled nineteen well-worn index cards from her purse, and separated them into three piles.

"Before you can transform an idea into a proverb," Sam said, pointing to each pile, "you need to choose a function, frame it, and top it off with a finish."

Cade looked at the cards slack-jawed. "Ah, sure," he said sarcastically. "That sounds straightforward enough."

"I know. So, let's start with something simpler. Instead of creating a new proverb, what if we reverse engineered one? We'll start with *a barking dog seldom bites*." Sam touched the first pile to reveal three index cards.

"Wait a minute," Cade asked. "Out of all Mr. Kemper's proverbs, you only found three function categories?"

"Yup. Definitions, predictions, and prescriptions."

Unconvinced, Cade asked, "Okay, what's a definition proverb?"

"Exactly like it sounds. Definition proverbs define one thing in terms of another. Typical

definition proverbs contain words like *is* and *are*."
You of all people should recognize that definition
proverbs in their purest forms are metaphors."

Cade studied the proverb for its metaphoric
roots. "While it's tempting to think that this proverb
is about dogs," Cade said, sounding very
professorial, "the proverb has more to do with
human nature. It's based on the metaphor *people are
dogs*. People, like dogs, can be affectionate, docile,
and aggressive. And while both people and dogs
cause pain, each does so differently. While people
can hurt you both physically and mentally, dogs
typically inflict their pain through biting."

"And don't forget, both can be loud," Sam said.

"Excellent point, Sam. So, *a barking dog seldom bites*
has two metaphoric roots. *People are dogs* and *loud is
dangerous*. Therefore, if *barking* is loud and *biting*
causes pain, then our instinct is to assume that loud
people and loud dogs are dangerous."

"Okay, I get definition proverbs," Tina said.
"What about predictions and prescriptions?"

"A predictive proverb illustrates a cause and
effect relationship—usually showing how one event
leads to another. And prescriptive proverbs suggest
ways to solve problems."

"Then *a barking dog seldom bites* is predictive," Tina

said. "The author wants to break our belief that *loud is dangerous* by suggesting that not all dogs bite. Some dogs—or people—use their barks as a ruse to project danger. In other words, don't worry because *his bark is worse than his bite.*"

"Hey, that's another way of saying the same thing," Cade said.

"It is," Sam agreed, "which brings up something that I learned while going through this process. I stumbled upon the concept of *proverb families*: proverbs that share the same metaphorical roots, but their delivery mechanisms differ. While *a barking dog seldom bites* is predictive, *his bark is worse than his bite* defines. As you can see, they have different functions. And that brings us to frames."

She spread the second pile to reveal five index cards. "A frame is something to build a proverb on. It adds structure to a definition, prediction, or a prescription. While going through Mr. Kemper's list, I found five frame types: metaphoric, comparisons, conditionals, derivatives, and none."

Tina and Cade viewed Sam's index cards differently. Cade saw them through a philosophical prism by which to view metaphors and policies. Tina examined them from the perspective of function words. Both hoped that Sam's cards would help tie their respective theories together.

Sam continued. "Metaphoric frames are simply proverbs stripped to their base metaphors such as *appearances are deceptive,* or *ignorance is bliss.*"

"Metaphors rule!" Cade said.

Sam rolled her eyes. "Comparison frames offer ways to distinguish between things by using qualifying words like *better, worse, best, greater,* or *as good as.* And conditional frames establish logical choices through terms such as *if/ then, when, if you, when you,* or *he who.*"

Tina took the first guess. "So, *a barking dog seldom bites* uses a comparison frame, because the author compares barking and non-barking dogs."

"So, does *his bark is worse than his bite,*" Cade added. "The author has qualified a *bark* as worse than a *bite.*"

"But what if we looked at another in this proverb family?" Sam said. "What if I said, *beware of the dog that doesn't bark?*"

Cade took the first shot. "That's a prescriptive proverb because it's offering advice to prevent future pain."

"Yet, it too also uses a comparison frame," Tina said, "because we are still comparing dogs and their tendencies to bark or bite."

Sam performed a happy dance in her chair. "I hate to get all geeky on you two, but this is fun, right? We have three proverbs that are based on the same metaphors. Each has a different function, but they all share the same frame."

"Since we're getting all geeky, let's go wild," Cade joked. "How can you have no frame?"

"Hold that thought," Sam said, "because I want to study these three proverbs for their finishes first. Finishing is where you add flair and style to a proverb." She spread the third and final pile of index cards across the table. "There are five finishing categories: conviction, ellipsis, negation, poetic, and wordplay. She fanned out twelve index cards and let her pupils read them.

- **Conviction** sets the confidence level of the proverb through using words such as *always*, *sometimes*, or *never* as in: *sometimes blessings come in disguise*

- **Ellipsis** truncates proverbs to just the essential words—sometimes eliminating the verb entirely, such as in: *least said, soonest mended*

- **Negation** uses negative logic to make points through words like *no* or *not* as in *one swallow does not a summer make*

- **Poetic** finishes add to the memorability and repeatability of proverbs. There are five different poetic types to consider: rhyme, rhythm, assonance, alliteration, and consonance.

- **Rhyme** uses a collection of same-sounding word fragments such as *meet roughness with toughness*

- **Rhythm** arranges syllables such that they form a beat, such as in *nothing ventured, nothing gained*, which follows the beat pattern of one-two; one-two; one-two-three

- **Assonance** is like rhyme, where it uses repeating vowel sounds. While *time* and *nine* don't rhyme in *a stitch in time saves nine*, the two words are tied together through the common pronunciation of the long "I" sound.

- **Alliteration** repeats a consonant sound at the beginning of a word, as in *it takes two to tango*

- **Consonance** is like alliteration, yet the consonance sounds are found in the middle and end of words as opposed to the front of them, such as: *one day a rooster, the next day a feather duster.*

- **Wordplay** involves a clever use of words. There are four wordplay subcategories: associations, double-use, opposites, and reversals.

- **Associations** play with the relationships between word meanings. For example, *a clever hawk hides its claws* uses the association between a bird of prey and its talons.

- **Double-use** finishes repeat words to make a point, such as in *a friend to all is a friend to none*

- **Opposites** make their points paradoxically, through contradictory or metaphorical meanings, such as *one man's gravy is another man's poison*

- **Reversals** are like double-use finishes because they repeat words but differ by reversing their order. For example, it's *not the size of the dog in a fight*, but the *size of the fight in the dog*

Tina and Cade scoured the cards to identify the finish for *a barking dog seldom bites*.

"I don't see any," Tina said.

Cade shook his head. "Same here."

"Look a little closer," Sam encouraged. "It has to do with *barks* and *bites*."

Tina finally saw it. "There's an alliterative relationship *bark* and *bite*."

"Bingo!" Sam said. "And what about *beware of the dog that doesn't bark*?"

"This one has a negation finish," Cade said. "Rather than worrying about barking dogs, the author suggests that we should be more concerned with the quiet dogs that *don't* bark."

"Okay, now I'm ready to answer Cade's question about proverbs that have no frames. Constructing proverbs is a process of ruthless editing. You start with a big idea, choose a function, frame and finish. The goal is to create the most potent proverb using the least amount of words."

"Like?" Tina asked.

"Take the proverb, *nothing ventured, nothing gained*," Sam replied.

"Prediction," Cade said.

"With a negation finish?" Tina asked.

"Oh!" Cade blurted. "And since *nothing* is used twice, it also has a double-use finish.

"It's subtle," Tina said, "but since *nothing ventured, nothing gained* rolls off the tongue, might it also have a little rhythm?"

"You don't have to convince me," Sam said.

"And the author finished the proverb with ellipsis," Tina added. "So, this proverb has four finishes?"

"See what I mean about the editing process? *Nothing ventured, nothing gained* is a predictive proverb with four finishes: negation, double-use, rhythm, and ellipsis. So, what's the frame?"

The two stared at the cards silently.

"I don't see one."

"Me either."

"There is none," Sam said. "It was eliminated by

the ellipsis finish."

"How so?"

"All proverbs start with both function and frames. But sometimes, frames get lost during the editing process." She could see that they needed a little extra help. "Let's walk through the process to create this proverb. We start out with a big idea about the relationship between risk and reward. Perhaps our first proverb attempt says something like, *he who does not venture cannot gain.*"

"A prediction proverb," Cade blurted.

"With a conditional frame and negative finish," Tina added.

"Great. Now, what if the author applies an ellipsis finish to reduce the number of words to four: *nothing ventured, nothing gained?*"

Tina saw it first. "The frame has been eliminated," Tina said. "Or perhaps it's implied?"

"I like that," said Sam. "Technically, the proverb has no frame, but somehow our minds can fill-in-the-blanks."

Cade wrapped up the exercise. "So, *nothing ventured, nothing gained* is a prediction proverb, with no frame that's finished with ellipsis, double-use, negation, and rhythm."

"What do you think of my silly cards now?" Sam said.

"They're fun," Cade said, "like diagramming sentences."

"You're such a geek," Sam said.

"Have you thought of expanding them?" Tina asked.

"Expanding? How?"

"We've used your cards to reverse engineer a proverb, but, if your goal is to help people create their own, I wonder if nineteen cards are enough."

Sam winced. She'd invested so much time and effort coming up with the cards that she couldn't conceive of investing more.

Tina saw the hesitance in Sam's eyes. "You've put a lot of work into these cards, Sam, but if I were to sit down with them in their present state, I'd probably feel overwhelmed. The reason that this exercise worked so well tonight is that you were here to guide us. I think the cards need a way to guide solitary users through the proverb-making process."

Sam understood where Tina was coming from. She'd developed a prototype, not a product. If she expected her tool to stand on its own, she'd need to beef it up. "I could add bigrams," she offered.

"I like that," Tina said. "As a user, I could use bigrams as little proverb prompters."

"Proverb prompters," Sam said. "That has a nice ring to it."

As the three chit-chatted throughout dessert, Tina thought about Mr. Kemper. Here she was, talking with a Ph.D. candidate and a consultant about proverbs. Cade used proverbs for his doctoral dissertation while Sam had developed a tool for creating them. Mr. Kemper would have loved this conversation. Upon second thought, she realized that he probably already was.

Universality

The more things change,
the more they stay the same

Kwasi wiped his mouth with a cloth napkin. "That was a great meal," he said.

Tina smiled. "I'm glad that you enjoyed it. This is one of my favorite restaurants in the city."

Tina learned of Kwasi's insatiable appetite for Italian food when she started representing his Ghanaian import company five years ago. Whenever he visited, she took him to Boston's North End where they'd talk about family over appetizers, business during the main course, and wrap-up the meal with general chit-chat over some cannoli and espresso. That's when Tina mentioned her interest in proverbs.

"Ah, proverbs," Kwasi, said thoughtfully. "They play a big role in my country."

"Really?" Tina said. "What do you mean?"

Kwasi paused to frame his thoughts. "Before we get into the specifics, you need to understand some background about the Akans culture. You see, our society is built upon different hierarchies—some are official, like government agencies, while others are cultural. One of these cultural offices is called the Chieftaincy, an office that plays a vital role in a regional community. At the head of the Chieftaincy sits a Chief."

"Is a Chief a ceremonial function?" Tina asked.

"No. Chiefs play active and important roles in their regions. Their responsibilities are so vast that Chiefs require many advisors—people that specialize in subjects as diverse as land, palace, interior, treasury, and the military."

"So, they're like the presidential cabinet in Washington?"

"Yes, that's a good analogy. One of these cabinet members, if you will, is called the *Okyeame*, or loosely translated, the *linguist*. Linguists play an indispensable role because they're the communications conduit between the people and Chief."

Tina wasn't following. "Chiefs can't communicate directly with their people?"

"It's a cultural thing. Don't think of Chiefs like the ruler of an American Indian tribe. Instead, think of them as an embodiment of the region's ancestors—someone who speaks the language of the dead. The Chief speaks the language of the dead, the community members speak the language of the living, and the linguists translate between the people and the Chief."

Tina felt even more confused than she had just seconds earlier. "You mean the Chief and the people speak different languages?"

"They both speak my native language, Twi, but think of it this way. The people speak in simple terms. The Chief speaks in complex terms. Therefore, if a common person wants to communicate with the Chief, the linguist must translate. Any guess at what the linguist uses as a translation mechanism?"

"I'll take a wild guess. Proverbs?"

"You've guessed correctly," Kwasi chuckled. "And a linguist's responsibilities don't end there. In addition to Chieftain translation duties, linguists also mediate negotiations or disputes. Americans may consider the practice as odd, but we don't negotiate directly with each other in Ghana. Each party hires a linguist and the two settle the matter through proverbs."

"That's fascinating," Tina said. "My research has focused on a proverb's ability to pass wisdom from one person to another in a passive way—essentially as a side benefit. However, it sounds like proverbs play a more active role in day-to-day Ghana."

"Proverbs play both active and passive roles," Kwasi said. "Since negotiations frequently play out publicly, anyone, young or old, can come to listen and learn. So, proverbs are used both actively, to settle a dispute, and passively, to transfer wisdom to those in attendance. As a young man, I loved sitting in the crowd and learning from the linguists."

Tina wondered about the feasibility of communicating through English proverbs. She imagined herself as a linguist armed with Mr. Kemper's notebook. She wondered if she could use his proverbs to defend an argument. "I'm curious," she said. "How many proverbs are we talking about here?"

"One reference has documented about seven thousand of them."

"Seven thousand!" Tina blurted, causing Kwasi to flinch.

"Why? Is that a lot?" he asked.

"Considering the collection that I've been working with contains fifteen hundred, yeah."

"Well, I'm sure that a lot more English proverbs exist than that," Kwasi said.

"It appears that our cultures use proverbs differently, but are the proverbs the same? For example, we have an English proverb that says, *there's no such thing as a free lunch*."

"*Dee watɔ na watua ho ka*[24]," Kwasi replied. "Literally translated it says, *What you buy, you pay for*."

Tina tried another. "How about, *Measure twice, cut once?*"

"*Dee wobɛtwa no pɛpɛ no, wotwaa no pɛ a, na woawie*[25] which translates into *What you are going to cut more than once, if you had cut it properly the first time, you would have completed the job*."

Tina noted that both of Kwasi's proverbs aligned with her LIWC results—they delivered their messages through the present tense and second person singular pronouns. They also used Sam's categories: the former with a predictive function

---

24 Peggy Appiah, Kwame Anthony Appiah, and Ivor Agyeman-Duah, Bu Me Bɛ: Proverbs of the Akans (London: Clarke Publishing, 2008), 84.
25 Appiah, Appiah, and Agyeman-Duah: 84.

built upon a conditional frame with an opposite wordplay finish and the latter being a prescriptive proverb build on a conditional frame with no finish. "Okay," she said. "There's definitely overlap between English and Twi proverbs, but can you give me an example where none exists?"

"Perhaps one that's tied to a specific cultural reference," Kwasi said. He thought for a moment. "Okay, let's say that two linguists are mediating an argument. The first party has made a promise, but the second party doubts that the first party can honor that promise. A linguist may say something like, *Deε wawe kɔkɔ ka sε ɔbεwe koraa a, yεnnye no akyinnye*[26], which translates to *If the one who has chewed the crab tells you that he will chew the calabash, don't doubt him.*"

"Sure," Tina said, dryly. "That makes perfect sense to me."

Kwasi laughed. "That proverb requires a little cultural understanding. You see, a crab is a shellfish and a calabash is a gourd, so they both have hard shells. Hence, the proverb means: *He who has proved himself in similar situations shouldn't be doubted.*"

Tina appreciated how the cultural references were

---

26 Appiah, Appiah, and Agyeman-Duah: 84.

based on metaphor, describing one thing in terms of another. Just as dogs and people shared traits for loudness and the ability to cause pain, shellfish and gourds shared tough outer crusts. "Kwasi, you not only translated a very specific cultural reference proverb into a generic English version, but you did so using English proverb-making rules." She explained how his translation used a *he who* bigram and how the cultural references held the metaphoric keys to unlocking its proverbial wisdom.

The more she thought about it, the more convinced she became. Proverbs were indeed universal and Kwasi's non-European examples offered her an additional layer of evidence.

Now all she had to do was convince her agent.

SAM ALWAYS HAD a hard time sleeping the night before a big presentation. She found herself waking every hour, on the hour, and gave up by the time four o'clock arrived. Grigsby stirred when she switched the nightstand lamp on.

"He who rises late must trot all day," she said. The pug raised an eyebrow, blinked, and returned to his doggy slumber.

She reviewed the report that she'd sent to Ryan earlier. The only thing she lacked was a proverb that both explained her findings and could help Amy explain it to others.

She spread index cards across her bed, paying special attention to her newest suit: *Starters*.

Starters
is the
better to
he who
if you
in the
is a
is better
it is
of the
the best
what you
you can
you can't

She read each line until her eyes stopped on the last one, *you can't*. There it was, she thought—a prediction proverb, built upon a comparison frame, with a wordplay finish. A lot rode on this little proverb—not only her job but the fate of the entire company. She wrote it down, reread it, and smiled at the perfect proverb that described both Pentameter's problem and its solution. The more confident she felt, the sleepier she became. Sam yawned, burrowed herself deep below her soft covers. *"Failure is not an option,"* she said to herself before giggling. "What the hell have you done to me, Mr. Kemper?"

PENTAMETER SOFTWARE'S headquarters were housed in an old textile mill about twenty-five miles north of Boston. The company had occupied the building since it acquired Edu-Print Publishing about ten years ago. It was a marriage made in corporate heaven. Edu-Print, an on-demand educational publishing pioneer had the content, Pentameter had the software development chops, and the combined company had become one of the most successful K-12 education publishers in the nation.

"Ms. Tennet has already been notified and will be right down," the receptionist said after Sam introduced herself. That's when she noticed that Craig and Ryan were already seated in the lobby.

"Are you ready?" Ryan asked nervously.

"As ready as I'm gonna be," she said.

"Hello, again Sam," Amy said as she came down the mill's original wooden stairs. "I've been looking forward to your presentation."

Sam shook her hand. "Me too, Ms. Tennet."

"Please. Call me Amy."

The three followed Pentameter's CEO to a large conference room that overlooked the building's ancient millpond. The wooden floors, seasoned through a century of abuse, creaked as the attendees settled into their chairs.

Craig opened the meeting. "Ms. Kim has some ideas to share with you," he said.

"I'm all ears."

"I've found an Achilles heel in your project," Sam said. "One of the tasks is based on a bad assumption."

"So, Zenekas screwed up," Craig editorialized.

"Well, it's an easy mistake to make if you aren't familiar with this particular line of products," Sam said.

"And of course, we are more than qualified to…" Craig said.

Amy held up her hand. "Stop selling, Craig. I get it. What assumptions?"

Sam presented a Gantt chart. "You see this algorithm development task? The original schedule only allotted one week to complete it. If I were the project manager, I'd have recommended at least a month. Unfortunately, the milestone slipped. Normally, such a slip wouldn't impact the schedule significantly, but since this task is the cog in the entire project's critical path, all of these downstream tasks are dependent upon its completion. As a result, most of the Santiago team is sitting idle waiting for its completion."

"Why didn't the project manager do something to help?" Amy asked.

"He did, sort of, by adding more people to the task. Unfortunately, those additional people exacerbated the problem instead."

"How so?" Amy probed.

"Adding resources can't fix this particular problem." Sam let the statement hang in the air for a moment. She'd just described the problem using technical terms like dependencies and probabilities and now was the time to drop her prepared proverb. *You can't hire nine consultants and have a baby in a month.*

Amy showed no emotion. Craig fought back a scowl. Ryan understood the inside joke and smiled.

The pregnant pause proved greater than Craig's ability to tolerate it. "Umm…what I think Ms. Kim means is…"

"I understand what Sam means," Amy interrupted. "So, how do we fix it?"

"I see that Charli Simmons is the software engineer on the task," Sam said. "I've worked with her. She's very good—if you leave her alone," Sam qualified. "My gut tells me that all of this *extra help*," she said, emphasizing the term with air quotes, "is driving her nuts."

"And removing this *extra help*," Amy mimicked Sam's air quotes gesture, "will ensure that we hit our original completion date?"

Sam answered before Craig could. "I can only guarantee that the shortest route to completing this project goes through Charli. If I were her project manager, I'd give her some room to think."

"And if I made you her project manager right now, what else would you do?"

"I'd rework the task dependencies to minimize the number of people waiting for her to complete that algorithm."

"The customer is breathing down our necks, Sam. He wants answers. Can we make up for lost time and still hit the original delivery date?"

Craig wanted to speak but exhibited remarkable self-restraint.

"There's no slack left in that schedule, Amy. But, we still have a shot at completing it in a few months."

Amy reviewed Sam's recommendations in silence. She considered milestones, dependencies, delivery dates, and the next meeting with her anxious customer. "Well, I may not be able to hire nine consultants and have a baby in a month," Amy said, "but I can hire one consultant to help with its birth. Welcome back, Sam."

RYAN CAUGHT UP with Sam in the parking lot. "Great job in there. Loved the proverb."

"A prediction proverb on a comparison frame with a wordplay finish."

"Not sure what that means, but I don't care. We're back in the game. Do you really think that we can finish in a few months?

"It's possible. I just need to speak to Charli. The rest will require some calculated risks and a little bit of luck."

"No nine consultants?" Ryan said.

"Nope," she said. *"You can't plant in the summer and expect to catch up by cramming in the fall."*

Go Forth and Proverb

Success comes from hard work

Tina arrived at the local diner a few minutes late. She found Sam already sitting at a table. "I just ordered you a cup of coffee," Sam said as Tina slipped into the booth.

"Thanks. How'd the big meeting go?"

"A proverb saved the day again!" She explained the situation, careful not to reveal any confidential information. "I summed up my analysis with *you can't hire nine consultants and have a baby in a month.*"

"That's not one of Mr. Kemper's proverbs."

"Nope. I used my cards."

"How are they coming, by the way?"

"Good. Bigrams came in handy just as you suggested. *You can't* is the prompt that led me to the proverb."

"Congrats," Tina said. "I've had a little breakthrough myself."

"Oh?"

Tina described her conversation with Kwasi. "He just sent me this book filled with over seven-thousand Ghanaian proverbs."

"Wait. Seven-thousand?"

"Makes Mr. Kemper's list look puny, right?"

"Do they all evaluate?"

"From what I can tell, yes."

"And what about functions, frames, and finishes?"

"Very similar. Their functions define, predict or prescribe and they appear to be built upon the same frames. The only parts that don't correlate very well are the finishes, which might have more to do with language translation than anything else. I'd need to spend more time with a native Twi speaker to understand those nuances."

"But, it sounds like you've found the evidence that you were looking for. Proverbs are universal across cultures."

"While seven-thousand African proverbs increased my confidence in the theory, I needed one last piece to bring it home—an ancient proverb that's found in multiple languages."

"From the grin on your face, I can see that you've found it?"

"The Golden Rule: *Do unto others as you would have them do unto you.*"

"Nice," Sam said. "A prescriptive proverb built upon a conditional frame with a double-use finish."

"I did a little research. Evidently, The Golden Rule is both old and cross-cultural. Ancient versions exist in Egypt, China and have even been found written in Sanskrit in India.[27] "

"And the ultimate litmus test," Sam said. "Does the Golden Rule exist among those seven-thousand Ghanaian proverbs?

Tina opened the book to a bookmarked page. "I have no idea about the pronunciation but take a look at this."

Sam read the text highlighted in yellow. *Obi nhyira ne ho na ɔmmɔ ne yɔnko dua.*[28]

"I see what you mean," Sam said, wryly. "I have no idea how to pronounce a backward 'c.'"

---

27 https://en.wikipedia.org/wiki/Golden_Rule
28 Appiah, Appiah, and Agyeman-Duah: 35 (Proverb 513).

"The proverb translates as, *Someone does not bless himself and curse his companion*. In other words, *Do as you would be done by*."

"The Golden Rule!"

"The fact that the Golden Rule is found in both European and non-European languages supports Mr. Kemper's assertion that proverbs are indeed universal. Adding Cade's thoughts that all humans use metaphor to both understand and share what they've learned strengthens his argument. And finally, I find it poetic that this last example teaches one of the most valuable traits of the human condition: empathy."

"Don't judge a man until you have walked a mile in his shoes," Sam said smugly.

"Look at you, Samantha Kim. When I first met you on that elevator, you couldn't even say, 'Hi.' Today, you're a proverbs expert."

It had been a long journey. A few months ago, Sam was oblivious to proverbs. Today, she not only used them in everyday life, but she'd built a practical tool to create them. But, she still saw Tina as the expert and waited like a dutiful student for her to impart one more piece of proverbial wisdom. It soon became apparent that Sam would be waiting for an eternity. "Wait. That's it? I'm done?"

"I wish it were that easy. I've been doing this for twenty years, Sam, and I'm still learning. Every time I hear a proverb, old or new, I realize how much more there is to learn. And whenever I think that I've learned everything there is to know about proverbs, I meet people like you and Cade who remind me how much I still don't know."

"I'm so grateful, Tina. How can I ever repay you?"

"Just continue Mr. Kemper's work, Sam. Go forth and proverb."

CADE SCANNED THE thinly populated auditorium for friendly faces. Unlike other universities, he'd chosen one with a tradition of inviting the public to attend dissertation defenses. He saw Sam and Tina sitting next to one another, acknowledged them with a wink, and began his presentation.

"I propose that proverbs are heuristics, mental shortcuts that help us make better life decisions— linguistic devices, used by the experienced to pass wisdom onto the less experienced through an economical use of simple words encoded with deep meaning.

"That's what makes proverbs such a special

communication device. Not only do listeners accept them readily, which is amazing considering how open we all are to accept advice," he said, getting a few laughs, "but once accepted, proverbs initiate a complex cognitive process within the listener's mind that both extracts and stores that advice.

"The simplicity of their presentation lies in stark contrast to the complexity of their function. Proverbs are both objective and subjective. They contain both premise and conclusion. They are accepted generally yet applied specifically. They derive their power from both logic and emotion and therefore benefit from both art and science to use inductive and deductive reasoning while delivering their wisdom through literary devices such as symbolism, alliteration, rhyme, and rhythm.

"Metaphor forms the heart of a proverb. When we say *time is money, the journey is the reward* or *orange is the new black*, we aren't saying these things literally. We're using common frames of reference to impart a deeper understanding of the world around us. These core understandings, borne through the experiences of everyday human existence, set a common foundation of understanding that underlies their ability to transfer wisdom. In other words, proverbs help listeners bootstrap basic human metaphorical understanding of the world to higher levels of abstraction that can ultimately lead to a better life.

"In conclusion, I propose that proverbs are the definitive link between teaching and learning and that they've been used throughout human history, independent of culture, creed, or political beliefs. Their success has contributed directly to a thriving human species. Thank you."

Sam wanted to applaud but didn't know if that'd be appropriate. The fact that the review board started asking questions immediately afterward proved that she'd made the right call. After about fifteen minutes, the Advisor asked one final question. "So, Cade. Where do you think this all leads?"

Sam squeezed Tina's arm. This would be exactly the wrong time for Cade to spiral off onto one of his anti-technology tangents. He took what felt like an eternity to answer.

"Recently, I've worried about the societal effects of our communications technologies. We use our portable media devices to receive, create, and transmit information. I was concerned that this always-on access to information was somehow making us insular and anti-communicative. But, proverbs have changed my pessimistic outlook. I think about how overwhelming it must have been for our predecessors to convert their thoughts into meaning through rudimentary language. They didn't know how to use the innovation of language back then, just as we don't know how to use our relatively new communications technologies today. But, our ancestors learned—first adding complexity to their languages and then honing that complexity using metaphors, proverbs, fables, allegories, and parables. I guess, in answer to your question, I have more hope that we'll do the same thing today. We'll adapt."

A light applause rewarded Cade's decent from the podium. He shook hands with his professors, board members, and ultimately the Advisor. "Nice job, she said. "I knew you could do it."

"I'm glad one of us did," he joked. "Thanks for being patient with me."

Sam greeted him with a bear hug. "Nice job, Doc."

"Let's not get ahead of ourselves," he said.

"Mr. Kemper would have loved this," Tina said. "He never could have imagined how some old notebook scribbles could lead to something so spectacular."

Jenn inched forward, put her arms around Cade

and gave him a kiss. "Congrats, Americano."

Sam's eyes widened. "Well, it looks like the Doc finally asked the girl out. I don't know which is more impressive, your dissertation or that you have a girlfriend," she joked.

"Well," Cade said. "A wise woman once explained the prescriptive qualities of faint hearts and fair ladies."

THE DINNER RESERVATION was for five: Sam, Cade, Jenn, Tina and her husband, Tom Jowett.

"What are we celebrating?" the waiter asked as he removed the tin foil from the top of a champagne bottle.

Jenn put her hand on Cade's shoulder. "This guy just earned his Ph.D."

"And this woman," Sam said, pointing to Tina, "just published her first book."

"That's a lot of celebrating, he said. "Congratulations to you both." The waiter poured champagne into each guest's glass and then disappeared into the crowded restaurant.

Sam raised her glass. "To my two friends. May the

fruits of your efforts bring you wild success. I'm so proud of both of you."

"Here, here," Tom said before everyone tapped their champagne flutes gently.

Tina stood. "And I have a very special announcement to make." Tom suddenly looked very uncomfortable. "Oh, don't worry, honey," Tina said. "It's about Sam."

"Whew!" Tom said, wiping mock sweat from his brow.

"I showed my publisher Sam's ratty old index cards. He wants to talk with you about publishing them."

Jenn held up her glass. "To Sam's cards."

Sam looked around the table and realized that this very moment was the culmination of a series of events that began with an exploding projector bulb. "I'd like to make one last toast," she said. "To Mr. Kemper. *You don't need lots of words to convey lots of meaning.*"

JUSTIN WRAPPED his presentation at the All-hands meeting by flashing his boyish smile and saying, "And that's the way the cookie crumbles." After an awkward silence, he asked the obligatory,

"Any questions?" A din of silence filled the room for the second time, so he tried to frame a face-saving exit. "Okay then, I'll hand the mic over to Sam who'll…"

"…explain how machine learning can help you shrink project schedules," she preempted.

It had been almost a year since Sam helped win Pentameter back. During that time, her team had developed a series of machine learning tools for schedule acceleration. Although the field test results were mixed, the trend was positive enough for Craig to authorize her to spread the practice more broadly within Atamaq.

Sam took command of the room which felt very different from her exploding-bulb presentation. She made definitive statements in the present tense and used the second person pronoun liberally. The audience's present-obsessed brains listened intently for ideas that would both protect and preserve their jobs.

A young man approached Sam after her talk. "Ms. Kim," he said timidly.

"Please, call me Sam. What's your name?"

"Aamir," he said. "I just wanted to tell you how much I enjoyed your presentation. You're such a good speaker."

"Thanks, Aamir, but that wasn't always the case. You shoulda seen me last year."

"Really? What changed?"

"Lemme ask you, Aamir. Do you really want to be a better communicator?"

"Yes?" he said, hesitantly.

"And are you willing to invest the time and effort required to do so?" she challenged.

"Yes," he answered with slightly more conviction.

Sam rummaged around in her backpack. "Then the first thing you need to do," she said, handing him a shrink-wrapped deck of what appeared to be playing cards, "is learn how to create proverbs."

*Wisdom is gained through experience
and conveyed through proverbs*

— Ron Ploof

Acknowledgments

Writing a book is a lonely process but you never write one alone. These pages were filtered through a team of players who listened, questioned, read, and advised.

Tamsen Webster was patient zero for my crazy idea to write a book about proverbs. Her instant and enthusiastic response catapulted me into a two-year trajectory through the fields of paremiology and linguistics. She's read everything, from the project's first ugly draft (and horrible name, BTW—make sure to ask me over a beer) to the version that you hold in your hands. It's not enough that I thank her. If you liked this book, you should probably thank her too at tamsenwebster.com.

While sharing my proverb obsession over a lunch with Kwam Ewusie, I learned about Ghanaian linguists. Two days later he sent me a book that contained 7,015 African proverbs. Before our conversation, I'd only collected Western proverb examples. <u>Bu Me Bɛ: Proverbs of the Akans</u> helped me uncover the fundamental truth that proverbs are universally-human devices used by all cultures, across time, distance, and languages.

Everyone needs a creative partner, someone who'll listen to any crazy idea without judgment. Mike Kilroy is that guy for me. My word-nerd brother and I meet at least once per month to share our *brilliant* insights over a pint (or three) of Guinness. We've attracted many an odd stare from bar patrons who've overheard snippets of these conversations of me detailing odd linguistic intricacies or Mike outlining his latest JFK conspiracy theory.

I first worked with my cousin-in-law/graphics guru, Michael Joe in 2015 when he masterfully transformed an Excel spreadsheet into a beautiful deck of cards that would become The StoryHow™ PitchDeck. I'm in constant awe of how he can transmogrify my foggy visions into sunny landscapes. When I requested book cover ideas, he sent me a proverb-inscribed brain. See what I mean?

Special thanks to those who read through countless manuscript versions: Ann Handley, Cathy MacPherson, C.C. Chapman, Don Ploof, John Wall, Jon Gordon, Karen Bartleson, Katie Wagner, Kim Mahady, Kip Meacham, Kwam Ewusie, Maribeth Cooper, Mike Kleine, and fellow storyteller Park Howell. Sharing early drafts of one's work is like handing someone your beating heart. Thanks to all for holding it so gently.

And finally, it's not easy being married to a writer. None of my books would exist without the support of my very patient wife, Tara. Thank you for enduring hundreds of hours listening to my caffeine-energized fingers pound a keyboard, followed by the rhythmic beat of my forehead smacking the desk. I love you.

About the Author

Upon hearing that he was a storyteller with a degree in electrical engineering, someone once asked Ron Ploof if he was a modern Renaissance man. "No," he responded. "I'm just a socially well-balanced geek." During his career in the high-tech electronics industry, Ron has designed control systems, provided pre-sales support as an EDA Applications engineer, AE manager, and sold chip design services as a business development manager.

But his first love has always been to communicate through storytelling. He once used a Hula Hoop to demonstrate a hemispherical resonating gyroscope to a large audience, explained mixed-signal simulation techniques using Lego® bricks and Velcro®, and sold $30 million in professional services by telling stories rather than riddling customers with PowerPoint bullets.

In 2005 he launched one of the world's first podcasts called, Griddlecakes Radio: Exploring the Lost Art of Audio Storytelling. He founded a social media consulting firm in 2008 and was the manager of social media for Epson America from 2012 to 2015. A prolific content creator, Ron has produced an audiobook about the American Revolution, written a job-skills book as a novel, wrote over 250 articles and case studies on B2B social media, wrote a book about B2B social media, and created The StoryHow™ PitchDeck, a deck of playing cards that helps business people convert their ideas, messages, and presentations into memorable narratives. Ever the storyteller, he even solved a personal 42-year-old mystery through his Project Lizzie.

Ron is a regular lecturer at USC Marshall School of Business. He's also lectured at UC Irvine, UC San Diego, Arizona State University, and at venture capitalist Tim Draper's school for young entrepreneurs, Draper University. He's spoken multiple times at the MarketingProfs B2B forum, along with Confab, Social Media Marketing World, Get Storied Conference, New Media Expo, and local chapters of Vistage and the Marketing Executives Networking Group.

Ron loves hearing from storytellers of all skill levels. Reach out to him at ron@storyhow.com.

Tina's Research

List of Literary Works that Proverbs Were Compared for Readability

1. Elementary Zoology	23. Pride and Prejudice
2. A Tale of Two Cities	24. Proverbs
3. Adventures of Huckleberry Finn	25. Pygmalion
4. Alice's Adventures in Wonderland	26. Rapunzel
5. Autobiography of Benjamin Franklin	27. Second Treatise of Government
6. Book of Genesis	28. Simple Sabotage Field Manual
7. Book of Proverbs	29. The Adventures of Sherlock Holmes
8. Common Sense	30. The Adventures of Tom Sawyer
9. Declaration of Independence	31. The Call of the Wild
10. Dr. Jekyll and Mr. Hyde	32. The Cat in the Hat
11. Dracula	33. The Jungle Book
12. Dubliners	34. The Kama Sutra of Vatsyayana
13. Frankenstein	35. The Narrative of the Life of Frederick Douglass
14. Great Expectations	36. The Red Badge of Courage
15. Hanzel and Gretel	37. The Republic
16. If You Give a Mouse a Cookie	38. The Time Machine
17. Leaves of Grass	39. Treasure Island
18. Little Red Riding Hood	40. Uncle Tom's Cabin
19. Metamorphosis	41. US Constitution
20. Moby Dick	42. Utopia
21. On The Duty Of Civil Disobedience	43. War and Peace
22. Paradise Lost	44. Wuthering Heights

List of Works that Proverbs
Were Compared with for LIWC Results

1. A Tale of Two Cities	26. On The Duty Of Civil Disobedience
2. Adventures of Huckleberry Finn	27. Paradise Lost
3. Alice's Adventures in Wonderland	28. Pride and Prejudice
4. Autobiography of Benjamin Franklin	29. Pygmalion
5. Blogs*	30. Rapunzel
6. Book of Genesis	31. Second Treatise of Government
7. Book of Proverbs	32. Simple Sabotage Field Manual
8. Common Sense	33. The Adventures of Sherlock Holmes
9. Declaration of Independence	34. The Adventures of Tom Sawyer
10. Dr. Jekyll and Mr. Hyde	35. The Call of the Wild
11. Dracula	36. The Cat in the Hat
12. Dubliners	37. The Jungle Book
13. Expressive writing *	38. The Kama Sutra of Vatsyayana
14. Frankenstein	39. The Narrative of the Life of Frederick Douglass
15. Grand Means *	40. The Red Badge of Courage
16. Great Expectations	41. The Republic
17. Hanzel and Gretel	42. The Time Machine
18. If You Give a Mouse a Cookie	43. Treasure Island
19. Leaves of Grass	44. Twitter *
20. Little Red Riding Hood	45. Uncle Tom's Cabin
21. Metamorphosis	46. US Constitution
22. Moby Dick	47. Utopia
23. Natural Speech *	48. War and Peace
24. Novels *	49. Wuthering Heights
25. NY Times *	* Data from pre-calculated LIWC values

Selected Gunning FOG Scores:
Proverbs vs. Other Works

Literary Work	Gunning Fog
Cat in the Hat	2.95
Proverbs	4.76
If You Give a Mouse a Cookie	5.75
Little Red Riding Hood	7.52
The Adventures of Tom Sawyer	7.87
Huckleberry Finn	8.66
Treasure Island	8.73
Hansel and Gretel	9.39
Cinderella	10.14
Book of Genesis	10.69
Pride & Prejudice	10.81
The Kama Sutra of Vatsyayana	10.74
Book of Proverbs (from the bible)	10.92
The New York Times	11.5*
Sleeping Beauty	13.06
US Constitution	17.22
The United States Declaration of Independence	20.48

* usingenglish.com

Top Ten Most Used Words
(English vs. Proverbs)

Word	Rank (English)	Rank (Proverbs)
the	1	1
be	2	19
to	3	5
of	4	6
and	5	9
a	6	2
in	7	7
that	8	39
have	9	37
I	10	646
than	71	10
is	> 100	3

LIWC Categories Chosen for Proverb Analysis

1. achieve	25. filler	49. posemo
2. adj	26. focusfuture	50. power
3. adverb	27. focuspast	51. ppron
4. affect	28. focuspresent	52. prep
5. affiliation	29. friend	53. pronoun
6. anger	30. health	54. quant
7. anx	31. hear	55. relativ
8. article	32. home	56. relig
9. assent	33. i	57. reward
10. auxverb	34. informal	58. risk
11. bio	35. ingest	59. sad
12. body	36. insight	60. see
13. cause	37. interrog	61. sexual
14. certain	38. ipron	62. shehe
15. cogproc	39. leisure	63. social
16. compare	40. male	64. space
17. conj	41. money	65. swear
18. death	42. motion	66. tentat
19. differ	43. negate	67. they
20. discrep	44. negemo	68. time
21. drives	45. netspeak	69. verb
22. family	46. nonflu	70. we
23. feel	47. number	71. work
24. female	48. percept	72. you

Categories that Proverbs
Ranked in the Top Ten

1. Achieve (win, success, better)	3. Drives
1. Affective Processes (happy, cried)	3. Feel (feels, touch)
1. Articles (a, an, the)	3. Ingestion (dish, eat, pizza)
1. Bio Processes (eat, blood, pain)	3. Sadness (crying, grief, sad)
1. Certainty (always, never)	4. 2nd person (you, your, thou)
1. Common Adj. (free, happy, long)	4. Friends (buddy, neighbor)
1. Comparisons (greater, best, after)	4. Motion (arrive, car, go)
1. Health (clinic, flu, pill)	5. Body (cheek, hands, spit)
1. Money (audit, cash, owe)	5. Death (bury, coffin, kill)
1. Negations (no, not, never)	6. Differentiation (hasn't, but, else)
1. Neg. Emotion (hurt, ugly, nasty)	6. Time
1. Pos. Emotion (love, nice, sweet)	7. Anger (hate, kill, annoyed)
1. Reward (take, prize, benefit)	8. Common Verbs (eat, come, carry)
1. Risk (danger, doubt)	8. Quantifiers (few, many, much)
2. Auxiliary Verbs (am, will, have)	9. Cognitive Processes (cause, know, ought)
2. Present Focus (today, is, now)	9. Emotional Tone
	10. LIWC Dictionary Words

Categories that Proverbs Ranked in the Bottom Ten

Proverb Rank	Title
41	**Female References** (girl, her, mom)
42	**1st Person Plural** (we, us, our)
43	**Assent** (agree, OK, yes)
43	**Space** (down, in, thin)
44	**Sexual** (horny, love, incest)
45	**1st Person Singular** (I, me, mine)
45	**3rd Person Singular** (she, her, him)
45	**Words > 6 letters**
46	**1st Person Singular** (I, me, mine)
46	**Total Function Words** (it, to, no, very)
47	**Personal Pronouns** (I, them, her)
47	**Total Pronouns** (I, them, itself)
48	**Words Per Sentence**
49	**Conjunctions** (and, but, whereas)
49	**Past Focus** (ago, did, talked)
49	**Prepositions** (to, with, above)
49	**3rd Person Plural** (they)

Sam's Cards

	Building Cards
Function	Definition
	Prediction
	Prescription
Frame	Comparisons
	Conditionals
	Derivatives
	None (implied)
Finish	Conviction
	Ellipsis
	Negation
	Poetic
	<ul><li>Assonance</li><li>Consonance</li><li>Rhythm</li><li>Rhyme</li><li>Alliteration</li></ul>
	Wordplay
	<ul><li>Association</li><li>Double-use</li><li>Opposites</li><li>Reversals</li></ul>

Brainstorm Cards	
Focus	Roles
	Events
	Influences
Starters	Bi-grams

Tools

Readability Calculator: https://www.online-utility.org/english/readability_test_and_improve.jsp/

Text Analyzer: https://www.online-utility.org/text/analyzer.jsp/

Gunning Fog Index:
http://www.usingenglish.com/glossary/fog-index.html/

Linguistic Inquiry and Word Count:
http://liwc.wpengine.com/

Research

Project Gutenberg: https://www.gutenberg.org/

Quotes: http://www.goodreads.com/

Quotes: https://www.brainyquote.com/

Chieftaincy:
https://en.wikipedia.org/wiki/Akan_Chieftaincy/

Linguists:
http://www.refworld.org/docid/3f7d4d9931.html/

Selected Bibliography

Appiah, Peggy, Kwame Anthony Appiah, and Ivor Agyeman-Duah. <u>Bu Me Bɛ: Proverbs of the Akans</u>. Oxfordshire, UK: Ayebia Clarke, 2007.

Lakoff, George, and Mark Johnson. <u>Metaphors We Live By</u>. The University of Chicago Press, 2003.

Lakoff, George, and Mark Turner. <u>More than Cool Reason: a Field Guide to Poetic Metaphor</u>. The University of Chicago Press, 1989.

Mieder, Wolfgang. <u>Proverbs: a Handbook</u>. Greenwood Press, 2004.

O'Neill, Alice. <u>Proverbs: the wisdom of the world</u>. New York: Bloomsbury, 2016.

Pennebaker, James W. <u>The Secret Life of Pronouns: What Our Words Say About Us</u>. New York: Bloomsbury, 2013.

Taylor, Archer. <u>The Proverb, and an Index to the Proverb</u>. Folklore Associates, 1962.

Titelman, Gregory Y. <u>Random House Dictionary of America's Popular Proverbs and Sayings</u>: New York: Random House, 2000

The Proverb PitchDeck

Interested in a proverb-making tool based on Sam's cards? The Proverb PitchDeck will be released in early 2019. For more information, check out:

https://storyhow.com/proverb_pitchdeck

Made in the USA
Las Vegas, NV
22 August 2022

53768161R00118